Little Red Book
of
English Vocabulary Today

By the same author

Little Red Book Series

Little Red Book of Slang-Chat Room Slang	Little Red Book of Synonyms
Little Red Book of English Vocabulary Today	Little Red Book of Antonyms
Little Red Book of Grammar Made Easy	Little Red Book of Common Errors
Little Red Book of English Proverbs	Little Red Book of Letter Writing
Little Red Book of Prepositions	Little Red Book of Essay Writing
Little Red Book of Idioms and Phrases	Little Red Book of Word Fact
Little Red Book of Effective Speaking Skills	Little Red Book of Language Checklist
Little Red Book of Phrasal Verbs	Little Red Book of Perfect Written English
Little Red Book of Euphemisms	Little Red Book of Punctuation
Little Red Book of Word Power	Little Red Book of Reading and Listening
Little Red Book of Modern Writing Skills	Little Red Book of A Child's First Dictionary

A2Z Book Series

A2Z Quiz Book	A2Z Book of Word Origins

Others

The Book of Fun Facts	The Book of Motivation
The Book of More Fun Facts	Read Write Right: Common Errors in English
The Book of Firsts and Lasts	The Students' Companion
The Book of Virtues	
World Facts Finder	

Fun Facts: Science	Fun with Maths
Fun Facts: Animals	Fun with Numbers
Fun Facts: India	Fun with Puzzles
Fun Facts: Nature	Fun with Riddles

Little Red Book *of* English Vocabulary Today

Terry O'Brien

RUPA

Published by
Rupa Publications India Pvt. Ltd 2011
7/16, Ansari Road, Daryaganj
New Delhi 110002

Sales centres:
Allahabad Bengaluru Chennai
Hyderabad Jaipur Kathmandu
Kolkata Mumbai

Copyright © Terry O'Brien 2011

All rights reserved.
No part of this publication may be reproduced, transmitted, or stored in a retrieval system, in any form or by any means, electronic, mechanical, photocopying, recording or otherwise, without the prior permission of the publisher.

ISBN: 978-81-291-1807-3

Twelfth impression 2022

15 14 13 12

The moral right of the author has been asserted.

Typeset by Innovative Processors, New Delhi.

Printed in India.

This book is sold subject to the condition that it shall not, by way of trade or otherwise, be lent, resold, hired out, or otherwise circulated, without the publisher's prior consent, in any form of binding or cover other than that in which it is published.

PREFACE

This is an incomplete book. The adaptability and richness of the English language makes it an impossible task to compile such extensive vocabulary into a single book or dictionary. However, I have tried to put together the basic vocabulary that everyone should be equipped with, irrespective of one's age group or field of study. This book is the beginning to every reader who should now take over – maintain your own vocabulary exercise book as new words come into usage and some old ones become obsolete or branch out into new avenues of meanings. Add the *"Little Red Book of English Vocabulary"* to your storehouse of vocabulary. *Little Red Book of English Vocabulary* will equip you for a quiz and enable you to be an interesting conversationalist and public speaker. The book has two parts: WHAT YOU SAY and HOW YOU SAY.

The canon is clear and simple: develop the 'response-ability'.

Dr. Terry O'Brien

I dedicate this book to late Professor A. P. O'Brien, my father, friend, guide and mentor, who inspired me to the canon of excellence: re-imagining what is essential. And, of course, to all who value the proper usage of each word spoken or written.

CONTENTS

What You Say
1. Phobias — 3
2. More common phobias — 4
3. A collectiveness of collective nouns — 7
4. One word more: non-animal group words — 10
5. Animals – nouns of assembly — 11
6. Comparatives — 13
7. Internet etiquette: one word more — 20
8. One word more: American English — 20
9. Idiomatic usage — 25
10. Blog vocabulary — 28
11. Ranks, professions, occupations and trades — 33
12. Types of governments — 69
13. Words denoting places — 70
14. Metaphors — 72
15. Graphy words — 73
16. Phile words — 74
17. Miso words — 75
18. Mania words — 75
19. Others
20. Ologies — 77
21. Literary words — 78
22. Itis — 80
23. Types of people — 81
24. Common medical terms — 85
25. More words confused — 86
26. Potpourri — 94
27. And more — 100
28. Greek words — 104

29.	Food & cooking words	106
30.	Portmanteau words	110
31.	Synonyms	113
32.	Antonyms	116
33.	Distinctive names given to the young of animals	118
34.	Words denoting animal sounds	119
35.	Non-animal sounds	120
36.	Words pertaining to the church	121
37.	Adjectives	123
38.	Proverbs	126
39.	Words pertaining to war	131
40.	Foreign phrases	133
41.	Some important English idioms	139
42.	Some key business words	146
43.	General media terms	153
44.	Broadcast media terms	154
45.	Internet media terms	161
46.	Print media terms	173
47.	Spam vocabulary	176

How You Say

48.	Wit & wisdom of famous persons	185
49.	And more	194

WHAT YOU SAY

Phobias

Modern Phobias

Modern Phobias is a weird and wonderful complaint. The list here may introduce you to some you never knew you had!

Fear of bills	versurphobia
Fear of brands	nomenophobia
Fear of growing old	senecophobia
Fear of opening email	aperepiphobia
Fear of not having the remote control	bulliphobia
Fear of failure	cadophobia
Fear of going bald	calvophobia
Fear of going grey	canusophobia
Fear of politicians	civiliphobia
Fear of call centres	coetusermophobia
Fear of eye contact	donoculophobia
Fear of your boss	duxophobia
Fear of undressing	exuerphobia
Fear of using your mobile	frigensophobia
Fear of the unanswerable questions	illerogophobia
Fear of being put on hold	inanophobia
Fear of parking	insistophobia
Fear of fans	laudaphobia
Fear of reality television	magnufraterphobia

Fear of texting	verbaphobia
Fear of using wrong words	malvocophobia
Fear of nothing	nihiliphobia
Fear of one's wife	uxorphobia
Fear that everyone has a better mobile than you	obsoletophobia
Fear of escalators	scalaphobia
Fear of watching something on the wrong channel	pluracanophobia
Fear of commercial television	proscriptiophobia
Fear of junk mail	quisquiliaphobia
Fear of dancing	saltaphobia
Fear of watching soaps	sapophobia

More Common Phobias

These are some interesting and unusual words. Many of them originated in the fields of medicine and science. Some of them, however, are the coinages of witty journalists.

Fear of	Condition	Fear of	Condition
air	aerophobia	darkness	nyctophoia, scotophobia
aloneness	autophobia		
animals	zoophobia	dawn	eosophobia

Fear of	Condition	Fear of	Condition
anything	kainophobia	death	thonatophobia
new	neophobia	depths	bathophobia
bad men	scelerophobia	dirt	mysophobia
barren space	cenophobia	disease	pathophobia
blood	hematophobia	dogs	cynophobia
bridges	gephyrophobia	dolls	pediophobia
burglars	scelerophobia	eating	phagophobia
cats	ailurophobia	everything	pantophobia
change	kainophobia	failure	kakorrhaphiophobia
choking	anginophobia	doctors	iatrophobia
cold	psychrophobia	floods	antlophobia
contamination	mysophobia	fog	homichlophobia
corpses	necrophobia	frogs	batrachophobia

Fear of	Condition	Fear of	Condition
crossing streets	dromophobia	forest	hylophobia
dampness	hygrophobia	ghosts	phasmophobia
height	acrophobia	girls	parthenophobia
high objects	batophobia	writing	graphophobia
injury	traumatophobia	knife	aichmophobia
insects	acarophobia	lice	pediculophobia
robber	harpaxophobia	lightning	astraphobia
scratches	amychophobia	marriage	gamophobia
sin	hamartophobia	medicine	pharmacophobia
sleep	hypnophobia	money	chrematophobia
snake	ophidiophobia	name	onomatophobia
speaking	laliophobia	odour	osmophobia
strangers	xenophobia	open spaces	agoraphobia
string	linophobia	work	ponophobia
touch	aphephobia	pain	algophobia

Fear of	Condition	Fear of	Condition
thunder	astraphobia	railroad or train	siderodromophobia
time	chronophobia	jealousy	zelophobia
travel	hodophobia	responsibility	hypengyophobia
vehicle	amaxophobia	heat	dthermophobia
walking	basiphobia	ridicule	categelophobia
women	gynophobia	river	potamophobia

A Collectiveness of Collective Nouns

- A faculty of academics
- A stand of arms
- A conflagration of arsonists
- A park of artillery
- A belt of asteroids
- A culture of bacteria
- A poverty of pipers
- A festival of balloons
- A shower of bustards
- A bevy of beauties
- A flotilla of boats
- A cluster of bombs

- A blush of boys
- A shuffle of bureaucrats
- A flock of bustards
- A draught of butlers
- A rabble of butterflies
- A rainbow of butterflies
- A coalition of cheetahs
- An intrusion of cockroaches
- A roll of coins
- A cluster of computers
- A convocation of eagles
- A clashing of economists
- A pain of ex-wives
- An impatience of wives
- A caste of flower-pots
- A giggle of girls
- A cloud of gnats
- A pantheon of gods
- A wisdom of grandparents
- A cloud of grasshoppers
- A cluster of grasshoppers
- An arsenal of guns
- A battery of guns
- A bloat of hippopotamuses
- A crash of hippopotamuses
- An argumentation of historians
- A charm of hummingbirds
- A shimmer of hummingbirds
- A multiply of husbands
- An unhappiness of husbands
- A wealth of information
- A cache of jewels

- A mob of kangaroos
- A huddle of lawyers
- A colony of lepers
- A lounge of lizards
- A number of mathematicians
- A riches of matrons
- A gallimaufry of noises
- A superfluity of nuns
- A rope of onions
- An illusion of painters
- A ponder of philosophers
- A poverty of pipers
- A unkindness of ravens
- A descent of relatives
- A confraternity of smokers
- A quarrel of sparrows
- A disguising of tailors
- A pool of typists
- A spawn of umbrellas
- A mob of wallabies of wives
- A trip of wildfowl
- A plump of wildfowl
- A coven of witches
- A bond of women
- A clew of worms
- A swarm of sycophants
- A leaning of left-wingers
- An absolution of priests
- A press of journalists
- A consideration of judges
- A patience of saints
- A crash of computers

- An irritation of mobile/cell phones
- An anorexia of supermodels
- A smirk of estate agents
- An attitude of teenagers
- A decline of men
- An ascension of women
- An idiocy of reality television contestants
- A clinch of lovers
- A loneliness of long-distance runners

One Word More: Non-Animal Group Words

A company of actors	A shock or fell hair
A host of angels	A truss of hay
A claque of hired applauders	A hamlet of houses in a village
A sheaf of arrows	A panel of jurymen
A troupe of artiste	A bevy of ladies
A field of athletes	A rouleau of money
A hand of bananas	A rope of pearls
A batch of bread	An anthology of poems
Rooks of building	A posse of police to quell a mob
A sheaf of corn	A pencil of rays
A bale of cotton	A nest of shelves
A board of directors	A caffle or gang or cluster of stars

A chest of drawers
A clutch of eggs
A bunting of flags
A bouquet of flowers
A crate of fruits

A set of tools
A clump of trees
A stack of wood
A skein of wool threads
A tuft of grass

ANIMALS – NOUNS OF ASSEMBLY

a herd of antelope
a shrewdness of apes
a pack or herd of asses
a nest of ants
a cete of badgers
a sleuth of bears (sloth)
a swarm or grist of bees
a chattering of choughs
a covert of coots
a murder of crows
a litter of cubs
a herd of deer
a paddling of ducks (in water)

a flock or flight of birds
a sedge or siege of bitterns
a sounder of boars
a brace or leash of bucks
a herd of buffaloes
a drove or herd of cattle
a clowder of cats
a brood or peep of chicken
a labour of moles
a troop of monkeys
a barren of mules
a watch of nightingales
a parliament of owls
a yoke, drove or team of oxen

a team of ducks (in flight)

a gang of elk

a fesnyng of ferrets

a shoal, draught or haul of fishes

a swarm of flies

a skulke of foxes

a gaggle of geese (on ground)

a skein of geese (in flight)

a herd or tribe or trip of goats

a charm of goldfinches

a covey of grouse

a colony of gulls (breeding)

a down or husk of hares

a cast of hawks

a brood of hens

a sedge or siege of herons

a covey of partridges

a muster of peacocks

a nye or nide of pheasants

a flock or flight of pigeons

a wing or congregation of plovers

a school of propoises

a litter of pups

a bevy of quails

a nest of rabbits

crash of rhinoceroses

a building or clamour of rooks

a herd or pod of seals

a flock of sheep

a host of sparrows

a murmuration of starlings

a flight of swallows

a shoal of herrings
a pack or mute of hounds
a swarm of insects
a troop of kangaroos
a kindle of kittens
an exaltation of larks
a leap of leopards
a pride of lions
a stud of mares

a herd or bevy of swans
a sounder or drift of swine
a knot of toads
a rafter of turkeys
a school of whales
a pod of whiting
a pack, rout or herd of wolves
a fall of woodcock

ONE WORD MORE

A nest of shelves, a bale of cotton, a nest of machine-guns, a tuft of grass, a hand of bananas.

Comparatives

A simile is a figure of speech that indirectly compares two different things by employing the words "like", "as", or "than".

Even though similes and metaphors are both forms of comparison, similes indirectly compare the two ideas and allow them to remain distinct in spite of their similarities, whereas metaphors compare two things directly. A mnemonic for a simile is that "a simile is similar or alike."

- He fights like a lion.
- She swims like a dolphin.

- He slithers like a snake.
- He runs like a cheetah.
- She kicks like a mule.
- He flopped like a fish out of water.

In contrast, the following similes explicitly state the features that are predicated of each target:

- He drinks copiously like a fish.
- She walks as gracefully and elegantly as a cat.
- He was as brave as a lion in the fight.
- He was as tough as a bull.
- He fights like a lion.
- She swims like a dolphin.
- He slithers like a snake.
- He runs like a cheetah.
- She kicks like a mule.
- He flopped like a fish out of water.

In contrast, the following similes explicitly state the features that are predicated of each target:

- When he got the tools out, he was as precise and thorough as a surgeon.
- He was as brave as a lion in the fight.
- He was as tough as a bull.
- As bright as the sun
- As busy as a beaver
- As busy as a bee
- As busy as a cat on a hot tin roof
- As calm as a millpond
- As clean as a hound's tooth
- As clean as a whistle
- As clear as a bell

- As clear as crystal
- As clear as mud
- As cold as ice
- As common as dirt
- As cool as a cucumber
- As crazy as a loon
- As cunning as a fox
- As cute as a baby
- As cute as a button
- As cute as a cup cake
- As damp as the salty blue ocean
- As dead as a doornail
- As dead as the dodo
- As deaf as a post
- As delicate as a flower
- As dense as a brick
- As different as chalk from cheese
- As drunk as a lord
- As dry as a bone
- As dry as dust
- As dull as a dishwasher
- As easy as A.B.C.
- As easy as pie
- As fast as a racecar
- As fat as a hippo
- As fat as a pig
- As fit as a fiddle
- As flat as a pancake
- As free as a bird
- As fresh as a daisy
- As funny as a balloon
- As gentle as a lamb

- As good as gold
- As hairy as an ape
- As happy as a clown
- As happy as a lark
- As happy as Larry
- As happy as a rat with a gold tooth
- As hard as nails
- As hard as rock
- As high as a kite
- As hoarse as a crow
- As hot as a fire cracker
- As hot as hell
- As hungry as a bear
- As hungry as a wolf
- As innocent as a lamb
- As keen as mustard
- As large as life
- As light as a feather
- As light as air
- As likely as not
- As loud as a lion
- As lowly as a worm
- As mad as a hatter
- As mad as a hornet
- As mad as the march hare
- As merry as a cricket
- As modest as a maiden
- As much use as a yard of pump water
- As naked as a baby
- As neat as a pin
- As nutty as a fruitcake
- As obstinate as a mule

- As old as dirt
- As old as the hills
- As pale as death
- As pale as a ghost
- As patient as Job
- As plain as day
- As pleased as Punch
- As poor as a church mouse
- As poor as dirt
- As pretty as a picture
- As proud as a peacock
- As pure as snow
- As pure as the driven snow
- As quick as a wink
- As quick as lightning
- As quick as silver
- As quiet as a mouse
- As rich as gold
- As right as rain
- As round as a barrel
- As round as a circle
- As round as a sphere
- As safe as houses
- As scarce as hen's teeth
- As sensitive as a flower
- As sharp as a needle
- As sharp as a razor
- As sick as a dog
- As sick as a parrot
- As silent as the dead
- As silent as the grave
- As silly as a goose

- As sleepy as a koala
- As slippery as an eel
- As slow as molasses
- As slow as a snail
- As slow as a tortoise
- As slow as a turtle
- As slow as a wet weekend
- As sly as a fox
- As smart as an owl
- As smooth as silk
- As snug as a bug in a rug
- As sober as a judge
- As soft as a baby's bottom
- As solid as a rock
- As solid as the ground we stand on
- As sound as a bell
- As sour as vinegar
- As steady as a rock
- As sticky as jam
- As stiff as a board
- As still as death
- As straight as an arrow
- As strong as an ox
- As stubborn as a mule
- As sturdy as an oak
- As sure as death and taxes
- As sweet as honey
- As tall as a giraffe
- As tight as a drum
- As thick as a brick
- As thin as a rake
- As thin as a toothpick
- As timid as a rabbit

- As tiny as a grain of sand
- As tough as leather
- As tough as nails
- As tough as old boots
- As tricky as a box of monkeys
- As welcome as a skunk at a lawn party
- As white as a ghost
- As white as a sheet
- As white as snow
- As wise as Solomon
- As wise as an owl
- Worked as hard as an Alabama cotton picker

Unusual Similes

- As mad as a cut snake
- As fast as a rat up a drain pipe
- Flat out like a lizard drinking
- Round like a rissole
- Off like a pound of prawns in the hot sun
- Thin as a thermometer

And more: Disgusting like garbage
Entangled like spaghetti
Incredible like a dream
Smoke like a chimney
Drink like a fish
Sleep like a log

Internet Etiquette: One Word More

- NETHICS: Ethics on the net
- "BRB": Be Right Back
- The "Golden Rule" of Netiquette is..... Remember the human
- "Lurk before you leap" in cyberspace?: It's important to get the lay of the land before jumping in
- "Flaming" is ------ Sending derogatory email or "verbally" attacking someone in a chat
- A "Newbie": They are new to the internet or the chat room
- "You have pm": They have sent you a "private message" or email
- "Internet troll": Someone who participates in a message board or chat with intentions of disrupting it in some way
- "ACK": Acknowledged
- "HTH": "Hope this helps" "Happy to help"
- SCREAM: Write in all capital letters

One Word More: American English

Food and Drinks

BRITISH	AMERICAN
Bill	Check
Biscuit	Cookie

British	American
Canteen	Cafeteria
Crisps	Chips
Cutlery	Silverware/flatware
Electric whisk	Mixer
Fish slice	Spatula
Jug	Pitcher
Liquidiser	Blender
Pudding/sweet	Dessert
Starter	Appetizer
Sweets	Candy
A take-away	A takeout
Tin	Can

Sports And Leisure

BRITISH	AMERICAN
Adverts	Commercials
Cinema	Movie theatre
Draughts	Checkers
Film	Movie
Football	Soccer
Fruit machine	Slot machine
Interval	Intermission
Match	Game
Pitch	Field
Side	Team

Education

BRITISH	AMERICAN
Degree course	Major
Education authority	School district
Form	Grade
Grounds	Campus
Mark	Grade
Postgraduate	Graduate
Primary school	Elementary school
Public school	Private school
Reception class	Kindergarten
Revise	Review
Secondary school	Junior high and high school
Term	Quarter or semester
Year	Grade

Key Americanisms

Freshman	First year student
Sophomore	Second year student
Junior	Third year student
Senior	Fourth year student

Everyday Life

BRITISH	AMERICAN
Bookshop	Bookstore
Cash till/cashpoint	ATM

British	American
Chemist's	Drugstore/pharmacy
Cheque	Check
Corner shop	Convenience store
Current account	Checking account
Deposit account	Savings account
Grocer's	Grocery (store)
Jumper	Sweater
Newsagent	Newsstand
Note	Bill
Off-licence	Liquor store/package store
Pants	Underpants/panties/shorts
Pay in	Deposit
Post	Mail
Queue	Line-up/wait in line
Shop assistant	Salesperson/sales assistant
Shopping centre	(Shopping) mall
Till	Cash register/checkout
Trolley	Cart
Trousers	Pants
Zip	Zipper

Around The House

BRITISH	AMERICAN
Blind	(Window) shade
Camp bed	Cot

Clingfilm	Plastic wrap
Clothespeg	Clothespin
Cot	Crib
Cotton reel	Spool of cotton
Curtains	Drapes, curtains
Dresser	Hutch (a dresser is a chest of drawers)
Footstool	Ottoman
Hoover	Vacuum cleaner
Hosepipe	Hose
Loo roll	Toilet paper, bathroom tissue
Net curtains	Sheers
Pelmet	Valance
Plaster	Band-aid
Pram	Baby carriage
Pushchair	Trolley
Rug (light blanket)	Throw
Serviette	Napkin
Sette	Couch/sofa/davenport
Sideboard	Buffet
Spanner	Wrench
Tea towel	Dishtowel
Washing powder	Laundry detergent
Washing-up liquid	Dishwashing liquid

Idiomatic Usage

Wear many hats
If someone wears many hats, they have different roles or tasks to perform.

Mother wit
Native intelligence; common sense.

Clear the decks
When you clear the decks, you get ready for an important action and put away items that might get in your way.

Straddle the fence
To straddle the fence is to be indecisive, often to the point where it becomes painful not to make a decision.

Get the lead out
This is used to tell someone to hurry up.

Toss-up
A result that is still unclear and can go either way is a toss-up.

As rare as hen's teeth
Something that is rare as hen's teeth is very rare or non-existent.

Pick up the pace
To speed things up.

Roll the dice
To take a chance on something. 'Let's roll the dice and see what happens.'

Pigs get fat, hogs get slaughtered
This idiom is used to express being satisfied with enough, that being greedy or too ambitious will be your ruin.

Pay peanuts
If someone is paid peanuts, it implies that their salary is very low.

A lot on my plate
If you have got a lot on your plate, you are very busy and have commitments.

101
Meaning "First year introductory course" in US universities. The meaning has broadened in every day language to mean any kind of information for beginners.

Far cry from
This means that something is very different from something.

In the running
If you have a reasonable chance, you're in the running.

Go pound salt
This means 'Get lost' or 'Go away'.
 ('Go pound sand' is also used.)

Near the knuckle
If something is near the knuckle, it is bit explicit or too close to the truth for comfort.

Pick someone's brains
If you pick someone's brains, you ask them for advice, suggestions and information about something they know about.

Lose your rag
If someone loses their rag, they are very angry about something.

Lay of the land
The lay of the land is the way something is organised, runs, is arranged, etc.

Curdle your blood
If something is very frightening or disturbing, it curdles your blood.

Wallflower
Meaning 1: A woman politician given an unimportant government position, so that the government can pretend it takes women seriously, is a wallflower.
Meaning 2: A shy person who is not asked to dance is a wallflower.

Blue skies
An overly enthusiastic outlook or disposition.
The sales team had blue skies projections for their deals, although not many of those deals were signed.

Wee hours
Wee hours are the first hours after midnight.

Older than dirt
Meaning 1: Something or someone that's older than the dirt is extremely old.
Meaning 2: Something or someone that's older than dirt is very old indeed.

Run with the hare and hunt with the hounds
This means to be a member of or to support two groups that are at odds with each other.

Go down a storm
To say that something has been enjoyable or successful, you can say that it has gone down a storm. E.g. Last night's party went down a storm, it was incredible.

Older than the hills
Something or someone's that's older than the hills is extremely old.

BLOG VOCABULARY

- Biblioblogosphere: A humorous reference to the world of librarian blogging.
- Blaudience: The audience, or readership, of a blog.
- Blawg: A blog focusing on commentary about the law, generally written by a law professor, law student, or lawyer. A portmanteau of 'blog' and 'law.'
- Bleg: A blog entry consisting of a request to the readers, such as for information or

contributions. A portmanteau of 'blog' and 'beg'. Also called 'Lazyweb.'
- Blog Carnival: A blog article that contains links to other articles covering a specific topic.
- Blistless or B-listless: When a blogger becomes listless or apathetic about posting. It is also indicative of what will happen to the blogger's mailing list.
- Blog client: (weblog client) is a software to manage (post, edit) blogs from the operating system with no need to launch a web browser.
- Blogger: Person who runs a blog.
- Bloggies: One of the most popular blog awards.
- Blog Farm: A website constructed from a group of linked weblogs.
- Blog feed: The XML-based file in which the blog hosting software places a machine-readable version of the blog.
- Blog hopping: To follow links from one blog entry to another.
- Bloglet: A short blog entry or a series of random thoughts in a single blog entry.
- Blogoneer: A portmanteau of 'blog' and 'pioneer', meaning a person who blogs with an expert or pioneering attitude.
- Blogorrhea: A portmanteau of 'blog' and 'logorrhea', meaning excessive and/or incoherent talkativeness in a weblog.
- Blogosphere: All blogs, or the blogging community. Also called blogistan or, more rarely, blogspace.

- Blogroll: A list of blogs. A blogger features a list of his favourite blogs in the sidebar of his blog.
- Blog site: The web location (URL) of a blog.
- Blogsite: Sometimes confused with a simple blog or blog site, but a blogsite is a web site which combines blog feeds from a variety of sources.
- Blogsnob: A person who refuses to respond to comments on their blog from people outside their circle of friends.
- Blogstorm: When a large amount of activity, information and opinion erupts around a particular subject or controversy in the blogosphere, it is sometimes called a blogstorm or blog swarm.
- Blogstream: A play on the term mainstream that references the alternative news and information network growing up around weblogs and user driven content mechanisms.
- BlogThis: Pioneered by Blogger.com, Blog allows the reader to automatically generate a blog entry based on the blog entry he/she is reading, and post to his/her blog.
- Bloll: A troll who specialises in blogs.
- A blogger who exhibits adolescent tendencies and lacks basic social graces or good manners.
- Boreblogging: Writing about personal matters that are barely interesting even to the writer – preferably in a slightly bent fashion so as to make it fun to read in spite of the subject matter.

- Celeblog: A blog detailing the lives of movie stars, musicians, and other celebrities, much like tabloid magazines. They often feature embarrassing or revealing paparazzi photos.
- Collaborative blog: A blog (usually focused on a single issue or political stripe) on which multiple users enjoy posting permission. Also known as group blog.
- Comment spam: Like e-mail spam. Robot 'spambots' flood a blog with advertising in the form of bogus comments. A serious problem that requires bloggers and blog platforms to have tools to exclude some users or ban some addresses in comments.
- A non-public blog (e.g. behind a firewall)
- Fisking: To rebut a blog entry in a line-by-line fashion.
- Flog: A portmanteau of 'fake' and 'blog'. A blog that's ghostwritten by someone, such as in the marketing department.
- Gulog: A portmanteau of 'gulag' and 'blog'. Used when a blog is so dismal and depressing. It's as if it were written in a Soviet labour camp.
- K-log: aka 'knowledge log', a type of blog usually used by knowledge workers and posted on a company intranet for sharing company knowledge.
- Link Love: Linking to a site or blog, usually unsolicited, that you like, enjoy, or find useful.

- Log in, blog to, log out: A catchphrase referring to blogger style of activity.
- Milblog: Term for blogs written by members or veterans of any branch of service - Army, Navy, Air Force, or Marines. A contraction of military and blog.
- Moblog: A portmanteau of 'mobile' and 'blog'. A blog featuring posts sent mainly by mobile phone, using SMS or MMS messages. They are often photoblogs.
- Momosphere: Term to encompass blogs written by mothers. A portmanteau of 'mom' and 'blogosphere'.
- Multi-blog: Creating, maintaining, and running multiple blogs, simultaneously.
- Multi-blogger: An individual, business, or institution that runs multiple blogs.
- Plog: Political blog - blog containing mainly politically-oriented material.
- Podcasting: Contraction of 'iPod' and 'broadcasting' (but not for iPods only). Posting audio and video material on a blog and its RSS feed, for digital players.
- Scribosphere: Term to encompass blogs written by professional and aspiring screenwriters. A portmanteau of 'scribe' and 'blogosphere'.
- Shocklog: Weblogs to produce shocking discussions by posting various shocking content.
- Spam blog: A blog which is composed of spam. A Spam blog or 'any blog whose creator doesn't add any written value.'
- Slashdotted: The Slashdot effect can hit blogs or other website, and is caused by a major

website (usually Slashdot, but also Digg, Metafilter, Boing Boing, Instapundit and others) sending huge amounts of temporary traffic that often slow down the server.
- Splog: A term used to refer to a 'spam blog', made popular in 2005 by Mark Cuban.
- Storyblog: A term used to describe blogs used primarily to publish written stories and poetry, used for practice usually by aspiring writers.
- Vlog: A video blog.

RANKS, PROFESSIONS, OCCUPATIONS AND TRADES

A

- ABLE SEAMAN: A seaman who reaches a standard of skill above that of an Ordinary Seaman.
- ACADEMIC: A scholarly person, of a university, etc.
- ACADEMICIAN: A member of an academy, especially of the Royal Academy of Arts.
- ACATER: A person who supplies food provisions, e.g. a ships chandler. Orig. Fr. achateur, meaning buyer.
- ACCIPITRARY: A falconer.
- ACCOMPTANT: An accountant.

- **ACCOUCHEUR:** A person, not always a qualified physician, who assists women in child birth.
- **ACCOUTREMENT MAKER:** A supplier or maker of military clothing or equipment.
- **ACTUARY:** An expert in statistics, especially one who calculates insurance risks, a person who keeps public accounts of business.
- **AERONAUT:** A balloonist or a trapeze artist in the circus or music halls.
- **ALABASTERER:** A person who works with alabaster.
- **ALCHEMIST:** A medieval chemist who claims to be able to turn base metals into gold.
- **ALL SPICE:** A nickname for a grocer.
- **ALMONER:** Distributor of charity to the needy.
- **ALMSMAN:** A person who receives alms or charity.
- **AMANUENSIS:** A person who writes what another dictates (words or music) or copies manuscripts; a secretary or stenographer.
- **AMBER & JET CUTTER:** A person who cuts and polishes amber and jet for jewellery.
- **AMEN MAN:** A parish clerk.
- **ANCHORITE:** A male hermit or religious recluse.
- **ANGLE IRON SMITH:** A person who makes angle iron i.e. flat iron bars bent at right angles lengthways.
- **ANIMAL & BIRD PRESERVER:** A taxidermist.
- **ANKLE BEATER:** A young person who helpes to drive the cattle to market.

- **ANNATTO MAKER:** A person who workes in the manufacture of dyes for paint or printing.
- **ANNUITANT:** A person who receives an annual income, not from working e.g. pensioner.
- **ANTIGROPELOS MAKER:** A person who makes waterproof leggings.
- **ANVIL SMITH:** A person who makes anvils and hammers for blacksmiths.
- **APIARIAN:** A beekeeper.
- **APOTHEECARY:** A chemist, druggist, pharmacist.
- **APPRAISER:** A person who appraises the value of goods, i.e. a broker.
- **APPRENTICE:** A person who is bound to a skilled worker for a specified time to learn a trade.
- **APRONMAN:** A mechanic.
- **ARBITER:** A person who judges disputes.
- **ARCHIVIST:** A person who keeps records of historical value.
- **ARTISAN:** A skilled tradesman.
- **ARTIST IN FIREWORKS:** A person who prepares fireworks displays.
- **ASHMAN:** A dustman.
- **ASSAY MASTER:** The person who determines the amount of gold or silver to go in coins.
- **ASSAYER:** A person who determines the proportions of metal in ore.

B

- **BACK'US BOY:** A kitchen servant, (from "back of the house").

- BACKMAKER: A person who makes "backs", vats, tubs, a Cooper.
- BACKSTER: A baker.
- BAGMAN: A travelling salesman.
- BAND FILER: A metal worker in the gun making industry.
- BARBER: A man who cuts men's hair and shaves beards, a men's hairdresser.
- BARD: A poet or minstrel.
- BAREMAN: A beggar or pauper.
- BARGE MATE: A naval officer.
- BARKEEPER: Another name for a toll-keeper.
- BARREL FILER: A person employed in the gun manufacturing industry.
- BASIL WORKER: A person who workes with sheep and goat skins.
- BASKETMAN: A person who makes baskets, and furniture from wicker, also a person employed to empty the basket of coal being offloaded from the colliers into the barges.
- BATMAN: An officers servant in the army.
- BATT MAKER: A person who makes the wadding used in quilt and mattress making.
- BAXTER: A baker.
- BEAVER: A person who makes felt used in hat making.
- BENDER: A person who cut leather.
- BESOM MAKER: A person who makes brooms made of a bundle of birch twigs bound onto a handle which was a thicker and roughly straight branch of the same wood.

- BILL POSTER: A person who put up notices, signs and advertisements.
- BINDER: A person who binds items e.g. books, hats etc.
- BIRD BOY: A person employed to scare away birds from crops.
- BIRD CATCHER: A person who catches birds for selling.
- BLACKING MAKER: A person who makes polish for shoes.
- BLADESMITH: A swordmaker or knife maker.
- BLEMMERE: A plumber
- BLINDSMAN: A person employed by the post office to deal with incorrectly addressed letters and parcels.
- BLOCK MAKER: A person who engraves the blocks used in the printing trade.
- BLOCK PRINTER: A printer who uses wooden blocks for printing.
- BOBBER: A person who polishes metals.
- BONE LACE MAKER: A person who makes pillow lace.
- BONE PICKER: A person who collects rags and bones aka Rag and Bone Man.
- BOOK KEEPER: A person who looks after the accounts for businesses.
- BOOKHOLDER: The prompter in the theatre.
- BOOKMAN: A student.
- BOWLMAN / BOWLWOMAN: A dealer in crockery.

- BRACHYGRAPHER: A shorthand writer.
- BRAZIER: A person who makes or repairs household items made from brass.
- BRIDGEMAN: A toll keeper at bridges.
- BRIGHTSMITH: A person who works with tin.
- BRODERER: An embroiderer.
- BROGGER: A wool merchant.
- BROIDERER: An embroiderer.
- BROOM DASHER: A dealer in brooms.
- BROTHERER: An embroiderer.
- BROUGE MAKER: A shoemaker.
- BROWNSMITH: A person who works with copper or brass.
- BUCK WASHER: A laundress.
- BUCKLESMITH: A person who makes buckles.
- BUMMER: An army deserter.
- BUNTER: A person who collects rags and bones.
- BUSHELER: A tailor's helper.
- BUSKER: A hair dresser.
- BUSS MAKER: A maker of guns.
- BUTNER: A person who makes buttons.

C

- CADDIE: A boy who carries messages or who runs errands.
- CADGER: A beggar.
- CAFENDER: A carpenter.
- CAINER: A person who makes walking sticks.
- CAIRD: Another term for a tinker.

- CAMBIST: An expert in financial exchange, a dealer in bills of exchange.
- CAMBRIC MAKER: A person who makes a fine linen or cotton fabric called cambric.
- CANCELLARIUS: Chancellor.
- CANDLE MAKER: A person who makes and sells candles.
- CANTING CALLER: An auctioneer.
- CANVASER: A person who makes canvas.
- CAPILLAIRE MAKER: A person who makes orange flavoured syrup.
- CAPITALIST: An investor who provides private capital or wealth for the production and distribution of goods.
- CAPPER: A person who makes caps usually worn by the working class.
- CAPTAIN: A person in charge of a ship or a group of soldiers. Also a term for an overseer.
- CARETAKER: A person hired to take charge, especially of house or ship in owner's absence, or a person looking after public buildings.
- CARTOGRAPHER: A map maker.
- CARTOMANCER: A fortune teller who uses cards.
- CARTWRIGHT: A person who makes wagons and carts.
- CASHMARIE: A person who sells fish usually at inland markets.
- CASTER or CASTOR: A person who makes small bottles used for sprinkling salt, pepper, sugar etc.
- CATTLE JOBBER: A person who buys and sells cattle.

- **CHAIR BODGER:** A travelling chair repairman.
- **CHANDLER:** A candle maker or candle seller.
- **CHAPELER:** A person who makes and sells hats.
- **CHARWOMAN:** A cleaning woman.
- **CHASER:** An engraver.
- **CHEESE FACTOR:** A dealer in cheeses.
- **CHEESE MONGER:** A dealer in cheeses.
- **CHIFFONIER:** A ragpicker.
- **CHIP:** A shipwright or carpenter.
- **CHIROPODIST:** A person who treats diseases of the feet and hands.
- **CHOWDER:** A fish monger.
- **CHRONOLOGIST:** A person who records official events of historical importance.
- **CLAKER:** A magician or astrologer.
- **CLASSMAN:** A unemployed labourer.
- **CLOTH LINTER or PICKER:** A person who removed unwanted threads and lint from the finished material.
- **CLOTHIER:** A person who makes or sells clothes.
- **CLOWER:** A person who makes nails.
- **COBBLER:** A person who mends shoes and boots.
- **COINER:** A person who works at the Mint stamping out coins.
- **COLLIER:** A coal miner, a coal merchant or a person who works on the coal barges.
- **COLPORTEUR:** A pedlar who sells books, particularly religious books.

- **COMPOSITOR:** A person who sets the type ready for printing.
- **CONFECTIONER:** A sweet and candy maker.
- **COOPER or CUPPER:** A person who makes or repairs wooden barrels and casks.
- **COPEMAN:** A dealer in goods,
- **COPER:** A horse dealer.
- **COPPERSMITH:** A person who works with copper.
- **CORK CUTTER:** A person who works with cork.
- **CORN CHANDLER:** A corn merchant.
- **CORN CUTTER:** A podiatrist.
- **CORN FACTOR:** A middleman in corn deals.
- **CORN METER:** An official who measures and weighs the corn at market.
- **CORVER:** A person who makes baskets used in coal mining known as corves.
- **COSTER WIFE:** A female street trader.
- **COSTERMONGER:** A person who sells fruit and vegetables in the street or market.
- **COTELER or COTYLER:** A person who makese and repairs knives.
- **COTILER:** A cutler.
- **COUCHER:** A person employed in the paper making trade.
- **COUNTOUR:** A person who collects rates.
- **COUPER:** A dealer, usually in cattle and horses.
- **COUPLE BEGGAR:** An itinerant priest who performs marriages without licence or banns.
- **COUPLER:** A person employed in the coal mines coupling the coal tubs together.

- COURANTEER: A journalist.
- COWHERD: A person who looks after cows.
- CRIMPER: A member of navy press gang.
- CROFTER: A tenant of a small piece of land.
- CUTLER: A knife seller or sharpener.

D

- DAIRYMAN: A worker or owner of a dairy farm or seller of dairy products.
- DAY LABORER: A person who is hired and paid on a day-by-day basis.
- DELVER: A person who dugs ditches.
- DEPARTER: A refiner of precious metals.
- DEVIL: A printer's errand boy.
- DEXTER: A dyer.
- DEY WIFE: A female dairy worker.
- DISH THROWER: A person who makes bowls and dishes from clay.
- DISTILLER: A person who distills spirits, aka rectifier.
- DOG BREAKER: A person who trains dogs.
- DOMESTIC: A household servant.
- DOOR KEEPER: A guard, janitor, or porter.
- DRAGOMAN: A person who acts as interpreter or guide in Turkish or Arabic.
- DRAINER: A person who makes drains.
- DRAPER: A dealer in fabrics, chiefly woollen and linen cloth, and sewing needs.
- DRESSMAKER: A person who made clothing.
- DROVER: A person who drives animal stock to market.

- DRUMMER: A travelling salesman.
- DRY SALTER: A dealer in pickles, dried meats, and sauces.
- DUFFER: A pedlar (of cheap goods).
- DUSTMAN: A person who collects domestic refuse, aka janitor or garbage collector.

E

- EDGE TOOL MAKER: Blacksmith who makes knives and agricultural implements such as scythes.
- EGG DEALER or FACTOR: An egg or poultry dealer.
- EGGLER: An egg or poultry dealer.
- ELLERMAN: A person who sells oil used for lamps. Also known as an oilman.
- ELYMAKER: An oilmaker.
- ENGRAVER: A person who cuts or carves designs or lettering in metal or stone etc.
- ENSIGN: A commissioned officer in the navy.
- ENUMERATOR: A person who collects information for Census from the householder and records it.
- EREMITE: A hermit.
- ERITE: A heretic.
- EXCHEQUER: A revenue collector.
- EXCISEMAN: An excise tax collector.
- EYER: A person who made eyes in needles used for sewing.

F

- FABER: An artisan or workman.
- FABRICATOR: A maker.
- FANCY MAN: Nickname for a pimp.
- FANCY WOMAN: A prostitute.
- FANCY-PEARL WORKER: A worker using mother-of-pearl making buttons or fancy goods.
- FANNER: A grain winnower.
- FARANDMAN: A stranger or traveller, especially a travelling merchant.
- FARRIER: Shoeing smith
- FAWKNER: A trainer of falcons.
- FEATHER-DRESSER: A person who cleans and prepares feathers for sale.
- FEATHER-WIFE: Woman who prepared feathers for use.
- FEATHERMAN: A dealer in feathers and plumes.
- FEEDER: A herdsman.
- FELL MONGER: A remover of hair or wool from hides in leather making.
- FERONER: Ironmonger.
- FISH FAG: A female fish monger.
- FLAUNER: A confectioner.
- FLESHER: A butcher or tannery worker.
- FOOT MAIDEN: A female servant.
- FOOT MAN: A servant who runs errands.
- FOOT PAD: A robber.
- FOOT STRAIGHTENER: In watchmaking, a person who assembles watch and clock dials.

- FORGEMAN: Blacksmith or assistant,
- FOWER: A street cleaner, sweeper.
- FREEMASON: A stonecutter.
- FRESER: A maker of frieze, a rough plaster.
- FRIPPERER: A buyer and seller of old clothes.
- FRISEUR: A hair dresser.
- FRUITERER: A fruit seller.
- FRUITESTERE: A female fruit seller.
- FULKER: A pawnbroker.
- FUNAMBULIST: A tightrope walker.
- FURNER: A baker.
- FURRIER: A dealer, maker or dresser of furs.

G

- GABELER: A tax collector.
- GANGSMAN: A foreman.
- GAOLER: A jailer.
- GATER: A watchman.
- GATWARD: A goat keeper.
- GILDER: A person who applies gold leaf.
- GIRDLER: A leather worker who makes girdles and belts, chiefly for the army.
- GLASSMAN: A seller of glassware.
- GLAZIER: A glasscutter or window glassman.
- GRACE WIFE: A midwife.
- GRAFFER: A notary or scrivener.
- GRANGER: A farmer.
- GRAZIER: A person who pastures and raises cattle.

- GREEN GROCER: A fruit and vegetable seller.
- GROOVER: A miner.

H

- HABERDASHER: Dealer in small articles, eg. ribbons, needles, pins.
- HACKER: Woodcutter.
- HAMMERMAN: A hammerer, a smith.
- HANDSELLER: A street vendor.
- HANDWOMAN: A midwife or female attendant.
- HATTER: A maker of or dealer in hats.
- HAWKER: Street seller who cries his wares in town,
- HAYMONGER: A dealer in hay.
- HEADSMAN: Nickname for an executioner.
- HEADSWOMAN: A midwife.
- HOD: A bricklayer's labourer.
- HODSMAN: A mason's assistant.
- HOGGARD: A pig drover.
- HORSE COPER: A horse dealer.
- HORSE COURSER: An owner of race horses.
- HOSIER: A retailer of stockings, socks, gloves, night-caps, etc.
- HOSTELLER: An innkeeper.

I

- ICEMAN: A seller or deliverer of ice.
- IDLEMAN: A gentleman of leisure.
- IRON MONGER: A dealer in hardware made of iron. Also known as a feroner.

J

- JACK: A young male assistant,
- JOBBER: A buyer in quantity to sell to others, a pieceworker.
- JONGLEUR: A travelling minstrel.

K

- KEDGER: A fisherman.
- KNACKER: A dealer in old horses, dead animals. Harness maker, saddler.

L

- LACE DRAWER: A child employed in lace work, drawing out threads.
- LAGGER: A sailor.
- LAPIDARY: A person who cuts, polishes or engraves precious stones.
- LAUNDERER: A washer.
- LAUNDERESS: A washerwoman, a person who washes linen.
- LIMNER: An illuminator of books, painter or drawer.
- LINENER: A linen draper, shirtmaker.
- LISTER: A dyer of cloth.
- LOBLOLLY BOY: An errand boy.

M

- MADERER: A person who gathers and sells garlic.

- ♦ MAID: A female domestic servant. Class including scullery, kitchen, house, general, parlour, nurse, laundry, Lady's etc.
- ♦ MALENDER: A farmer.
- ♦ MASON: A stonecutter or stone-dresser.
- ♦ MELDER: A corn miller.
- ♦ MERCATOR: A merchant.
- ♦ MERCER: A cloth seller, chiefly silks and velvets.
- ♦ METALMAN: A worker in metals.
- ♦ METERER: A poet.
- ♦ MIDWIFE: A woman who assists in child birth.
- ♦ MILLINER: Maker of ladies, hats, bonnets, etc.
- ♦ MINER: A worker in a mine, digging for coal, ironstone, lead, tin miner, etc.
- ♦ MONGER: A dealer in goods (i.e., fishmonger, ironmonger).
- ♦ MOUNTEBANK: A seller of ineffectual patent medicines.
- ♦ MUGSELLER: A seller of cups, mugs.

N

- ♦ NEDELLER: A needle maker.
- ♦ NETTER: A net maker.
- ♦ NIGHTWALKER: A watchman or bellman.
- ♦ NIPPER: A lorry boy, a young person employed by the carter or wagoner to assist with the collection and delivery of goods.
- ♦ NOB THATCHER: A wig maker.

- NOTARY: A person officially authorised to draw up or attest contracts, wills, deeds, or similar documents, to protest bills of exchange.
- NOTERER: A notary.

O

- OCCUPIER: A tradesman.
- OILMAN: A person who sells the oil for lamps.
- OLITOR: A kitchen gardener.
- ORDERLY: A soldier who functions as a servant for an officer.
- OUT CRIER: An auctioneer.
- OVERLOOKER: A superintendent or overseer.

P

- PACK THREAD SPINNER: The operator of the machine which makes thread or twine.
- PACKER: A person who packs goods such as pickles or herring.
- PACKMAN: A pedlar, a person who travels around carrying goods for sale in a pack.
- PAD MAKER: A person who makes small baskets used for measuring.
- PALINGMAN: A seller of eels, a fishmonger.
- PANSMITH: A person who makes pans i.e. a metal worker.
- PANTLER: A butler.

- **PARKER:** The person in charge of a park, usually a hunting or game park.
- **PASSAGE KEEPER:** A person who keeps passages and alleys clean.
- **PASTELER:** A pastry chef.
- **PAVYLER:** A person who puts up pavilions or tents etc.
- **PAWNBROKER:** A person who loans money with interest against items of value left for security.
- **PEDLAR:** A person who sells things house-to-house or on the road.
- **PELTERER:** A person who works with animal skins.
- **PIECE BROKER:** A person who sells material remnants.
- **PILLER:** A robber.
- **PITMAN:** A coal miner.
- **PLOWMAN:** A farmer.
- **PLOWWRIGHT:** A maker or repairer of ploughs.
- **PLUMASSIER:** A person who makes or sells plumes, ornamental feathers.
- **PLUMBER:** A person who works with lead-installed or repaired pipes and drains of all types.
- **POINTMAKER:** A person who makes the tips of laces.
- **PORTER:** A person employed to carry baggage or attend to doors in public places. A door or gatekeeper.

- **PORTMANTEAU MAKER:** A maker of leather trunks for clothes, etc., opening into two equal parts.
- **POTATO BADGER:** A seller of potatoes.
- **POTTER:** A maker or seller of pottery.
- **POUCH MAKER:** A person who makes pouches or purses.
- **POYNTER:** A lace maker.
- **PRECEPTRESS:** A school mistress.
- **PRENTIS:** An apprentice.
- **PROCTOR:** The official of a university.
- **PUGGARD:** A thief.
- **PUMBUM WORKER:** A plumber.

Q

- **QUARREL PICKER:** A glazier.
- **QUARRIER:** A person who works in a quarry, a quarryman.
- **QUARRYMAN:** A quarry worker.

R

- **RAG GATHERERS:** A person (usually children) employed to clear the rags from the machinery in the mills.
- **RAG MAN:** A person who goes from street to street collecting and selling old clothes and rags.
- **RAG PICKER:** A person who sorts through the left over rags to find reusable ones.
- **REDAR:** An interpreter of dreams.

- REDSMITH: A goldsmith.
- RENOVATOR: A person who repairs clothing.
- ROCKGETTER: A rocksalt miner.
- ROPER: A maker of ropes or nets.
- RUGMAN: A dealer in rugs.

S

- SALESMAN: A person who sells things.
- SALOONIST: A saloon keeper.
- SAUCER: A person who makes or deals in salt.
- SCOTCHMAN: A person who sells goods door-to-door with payment to be made by instalments.
- SCULLION: A male servant who performs all the menial tasks.
- SILVERSMITH: A person who works with silver.
- SKIPPER: The master of a ship.
- SMIDDY: A smith.
- SMITH: A person who works with any metal.
- SMUGSMITH: A smuggler.
- SNOBSCAT: A shoe repairer.
- SOAP BOILER (SOPER): A soap maker.
- SOJOURNER CLOTHIER: A travelling clothes salesman.
- SOLICITOR: A lawyer.
- SORTOR: A tailor.
- SOUTER: A shoemaker.
- SPALLIER: A person who works in a tin works performing the menial tasks.

- SPERVITER: A keeper of sparrows.
- SPICER: A grocer or dealer in spices.
- SPINNER: A person who spins yarn or fabric.
- SPINSTER: A woman who spins; unmarried woman.
- SPLITTER: A person who operates a splitting machine or a person who splits things by hand e.g. stone, timber etc.
- SPOONER: A person who makes spoons.
- SPURRER: Maker of spurs.
- SPURRIER: A maker of spurs.
- SQUIRE: (See ESQUIRE) [1] A practitioner of a profession, [2] A magistrate or lawyer, [3] A country gentleman especially the chief landed proprietor in a district, [4] A knights attendant.
- STABLER, See OSTLER, STAINER: A person who colours glass or wood.
- STALLMAN: A keeper of a market stall.
- STAMPER: A person who operated a stamping machine.
- STAMPMAN: A worker of an ore crushing machine.
- STATIONARY ENGINE DRIVER: A person who operated a steam engine which was used for pumping water or sewage, or driving machinery in an industrial environment such as a factory, mill or mine.
- STATIONARY ENGINEER: A caretaker of machinery such as pumping engines or lifts/hoists. Also used later for a person who looked after the electrical and plumbing installations

in an apartment block or office block, aka Janitor.
- ♦ STATIONER: A bookseller, seller of paper and writing implements.
- ♦ STATIST: A politician.
- ♦ STAY MAKER: A corset maker.
- ♦ STEERSMAN: A ship's helmsman.
- ♦ STENTERER: A person who operated the cloth finishing machine.
- ♦ STEP BOY: A person employed to help passengers to enter or leave the coach.
- ♦ STEVEDORE: A dock worker or labourer who unloads and loads ships' cargoes.
- ♦ STICHER: A person who does decorative stitching.
- ♦ STOCKINGER: A person who makes stockings, or dealer in stockings. Usually, a dealer would be known as a Hosier.
- ♦ STOKER: A person who tends the fire of an engine boiler.
- ♦ STONE PICKER: A person employed to remove the stones from the farmers fields before planting.
- ♦ STONE WORKER: A person who works with stone e.g. masons, quarries etc.
- ♦ STONEMAN: A surveyor of highways.
- ♦ STOWYER: A person who stowed the nets away on fishing boats.
- ♦ STRAVAIGER: A vagrant.
- ♦ STRAW JOINER: A person who thatched roofs.
- ♦ STRAW PLAITER: A person who made straw braids for the hat industry.

- **STREAKER**: A person who prepares the body for burial.
- **STREET ORDERLY** or **BOY**: A street cleaner.
- **STRETCHER**: A person who stretches fabrics in the textile trade, sometimes called a tenter.
- **STRIKER**: A blacksmiths helper. The person who harpoones the whale.
- **STRINGER**: A person who makes the strings for bows.
- **STRIPPER**: A person employed in the woollen trade to remove the rubbish from the carding machines.
- **STUFF GOWSMAN**: A junior barrister.
- **STUFF WEAVER**: A person who weaves stuff, the coarse part of flax.
- **SUCKSMITH**: A person who makes ploughshares.
- **SUMNER**: A summoner or apparitor.
- **SUMPTER**: A porter.
- **SURFACE MAN**: A person who works on the surface of a mine.
- **SUTLER**: A merchant or peddler in an army camp.
- **SWAILER**: A miller or dealer in grain. A corn miller.
- **SWAIN**: A herdsman.
- **SWEEP**: A chimneysweep.
- **SWEEPER OUT**: A person employed in the mills to keep the floor clean.
- **SWELL MAKER**: A person who makes shallow baskets.

- SWINEHERDER: A pig keeper.
- SWORD CUTLER: A sword maker.

T

- TABLER: A boarding house operator.
- TACKLER: An overlooker of powerloom weavers.
- TAILOR: A person who makes or repairs clothes.
- TAKER OFF or TAKER IN: A person (usually a child) employed to unhitch the coal tubs from the endless rope system.
- TALLOW CHANDLER: A person who makes or sells candles.
- TALLY CLERK: A person who keeps count of goods arriving or departing from warehouses, docks etc.
- TALLYMAN/TALLYFELLOW: A person who sells goods that are paid for in instalments.
- TAN BARK STRIPPER: A person who collects the bark that is used in the tanning process.
- TANNER: A person who tans hides and skins to make leather.
- TAPER WEAVER: A person who makes the wicks for candles.
- TAPICER or TAPITER: A person who weaves worsted cloth.
- TAPLEY: One who puts the tap in an ale cask.
- TAPSTER: A person employed to serve the beer in public houses, a barman.

- **TARRIER:** A person in charge of a pack of terriers used for hunting.
- **TASKER:** A thresher or reaper.
- **TASSELER:** A person who makes tassels used in furnishings. A nobleman.
- **TAVERNER:** An innkeeper.
- **TAWER:** A person who makes white leather.
- **TEEMER:** [1] A person who empties grain from the cart. [2] A person who pours the molten steel into the moulds.
- **TENTER:** A person who stretches the cloth on a machine whilst it is drying. A person who looks after and maintains the machine used in the process. Also the term for a person who looks after something e.g. a door tenter or pony tenter in the coal mining trade.
- **TERRIER:** A person in charge of a pack of terriers used for hunting.
- **TEXTOR:** A weaver.
- **THACKER:** A roof thatcher.
- **THATCHER:** A person who covers roofs with straw or reeds.
- **THIRDBOROUGH:** An under-constable.
- **THRESHER:** A person who separates the grain from the husks and straw.
- **THROWSTER:** A person in the textile trade who twists the strands of fibre together into yarn.
- **TICKNEY MAN or WOMAN:** A person who sells earthenware from town to town.
- **TIDE GAUGER:** A person who monitors the state of the tide.

- **TIDE SURVEYOR:** A person who monitored the state of the tide.
- **TIDE WAITER:** A customs inspector.
- **TIEMAKER:** A person who makes wooden railway ties.
- **TIGER:** A small groom or pageboy in livery.
- **TILER:** A person who puts tiles in place either on the roof or floor.
- **TILLER:** A farmer.
- **TILLMAN:** A ploughman.
- **TILTMAKER:** A person who makes canvas awnings or canopies.
- **TIMEKEEPER:** A person responsible for making sure that things happen on time e.g. worker arriving or departing, trains, coaches, omnibuses, etc.
- **TIMES IRONER:** Servant responsible for ironing the daily newspaper.
- **TINCTOR:** A dyer.
- **TINKER:** A travelling salesman of pots and pans etc. or travelling repairman.
- **TINNER:** A person who works in the tin mines or a tinsmith.
- **TINSMITH:** A person who works with tin.
- **TINTER or TEINTER:** An artist who performs tinting.
- **TIPPER:** A person who puts the metal tips on arrows, etc.
- **TIPPLER:** A person who keeps an ale house.
- **TIPSTAFF:** [1] A court official. [2] A policeman.

- **TIREWOMAN:** [1] A milliner. [2] A hairdresser. [3] A female dresser, especially in the theatre.
- **TIXTOR:** A weaver.
- **TOBACCO SPINNER:** A maker of cigars.
- **TODHUNTER:** A person employed by the parish to hunt foxes.
- **TOE RAG:** A person who works at the docks as a corn porter.
- **TOILINET MANUFACTURER:** A person who makes toilinet (a kind of quilting).
- **TOLLMAN:** A person who collects tolls.
- **TONSOR:** Latin for barber.
- **TOOL HELVER:** A person who makes tool handles.
- **TOP SAWYER:** The upper man in a saw pit.
- **TOPMAN:** A sailor who works in the ship's rigging.
- **TOPSMAN:** The head cattle drover.
- **TOUCH HOLER:** A person who works in the gun manufacturing industry.
- **TOW CARD MAKER:** A person who makes tow cards, used in the textile industry.
- **TOWN CHABERLAIN:** A person who looks after the towns affairs.
- **TOWN CRIER:** A person who makes public announcements in the streets.
- **TOWN HUSBAND:** A person employed by the parish to collect the money from the fathers of illegitimate children for their upkeep.
- **TOWNSWAITER:** A customs man.
- **TOYMAN or TOY DEALER:** A person who sells children's toys.

- **TOZER:** A person who works in the wool mills employed to tose or tease the cloth.
- **TRADESMAN:** A shopkeeper or skilled craftsman.
- **TRAMMER:** A young person who works in the mines.
- **TRAMPLER:** A lawyer.
- **TRANQUETER:** A person who makes hoops.
- **TRANTER:** A peddler.
- **TRAPPER:** A young person employed in the mines to open and shut the doors for the miners.
- **TRAVERS:** A collector of fees at a toll bridge.
- **TREEN MAKER:** A person who makes domestic articles from wood.
- **TREENAIL MAKER:** A person who makes the long wooden pins used in shipbuilding.
- **TRENCHERMAKER:** A person who makes wooden boards or platters for serving food from or cutting and slicing food on.
- **TRENCHERMAN:** A cook.
- **TREPANGER:** A person who uses a circular saw to cut timber.
- **TRIMMER:** A person who trims a ship by re-arranging its cargo.
- **TROACHER:** A pedlar.
- **TROLLEY CARTER:** A person who operats the tubs in the mines.
- **TRONER:** A weighing official at the markets.
- **TROUCHMAN or TRUCHMAN:** An interpreter.
- **TROVER:** A smuggler.
- **TRUCHMAN:** An interpreter.

- TRUGGER: A person who makes long shallow baskets.
- TRUSSER: A person who bundles and ties hay, aka Hay Baler.
- TUBBER: A person who makes tubs and barrels, i.e. a cooper.
- TUBEDRAWER: A person who made tubes.
- TUBMAN: [1] A person who works the mines filling the tubs. [2] A court official. [3] An English barrister
- TUCKER: A cleaner of cloth goods.
- TUCKER IN: A maid who attends the bedroom and "tucked in the bedclothes".
- TUNIST: A person who tunes musical instruments.
- TURNER: [1] A lathe operator. [2] A gymnast, particularly street performers or beggars.
- TURNING BOY: A person who assists the weaver by turning the bar on the loom.
- TURNKEY: A prison warder or jail keeper.
- TWEENIE or TWEENY: A maid who works "between the stairs", she assists the cooks and the housemaids.
- TWIST HAND: A person who operates a lace machine.
- TWISTER or TWISTERER: A person who operates the machine used for twisting yarns and threads together.

U

- ULNAGER: A person appointed to examine the quality of woollen goods to be sold.

- UPHOLDER: [1] A person who makes quilts or mattresses. [2] A person who assists the auctioneer.
- UPHOLSTERER: A person who finishes furniture by putting on the padding and cloth.
- UPRIGHT WORKER: A chimney sweep.

V

- VALET: A male servant that attends a nobleman or gentleman.
- VALUATOR: A person who values objects.
- VASSAL: A servant of the lowest order.
- VATMAN: [1] A person employed in the paper making industry to put the paper pulp into the moulds. [2] A person who works with vats e.g. in beer and wine making.
- VENATOR (VENUR): A huntsman.
- VERDERER: An official in charge of the royal forest.
- VERGE MAKER: A person who makes the spindles used in clocks and watches.
- VERGER: A person who works with the priest in the running the church.
- VERRIER: A glazier.
- VESTMENT MAKER: A person who makes the gowns worn by priests.
- VICTUALER: A seller of food/drink.
- VIEWER: A person who worked at the mines in a managerial capacity.

- **VILLEIN**: A person who pays dues to the lord of the manor in return for use of the land.
- **VINTAGER**: A grape farmer, wine maker.
- **VINTNER**: A wine merchant.
- **VIRGINAL PLAYER**: A person who plays a musical instrument similar to a harpsichord.
- **VULCAN**: A blacksmith.

W

- **WABSTER**: A weaver.
- **WAGGONER**: A person who drives a wagon, a carrier.
- **WAILER**: A person employed in the mines to remove the impurities from the coal.
- **WAINWRIGHT**: A person who builds or repairs wagons.
- **WAITMAN** or **WAKEMAN**: A night watchman.
- **WALKER**: A cloth worker who cleans and thickens the cloth by wetting it, then walking over it.
- **WALLER**: A person who builds walls either with bricks or dry stone, also a person who works making coarse salt.
- **WANTCATCHER**: A person employed to catch moles.
- **WANTER**: A mole catcher.
- **WARDER**: A person in charge of prisoners.
- **WAREHOUSEMAN**: A person in-charge of a warehouse or one employed in a warehouse.

- **WARPER:** A person who sets the warp thread on the looms, also a person employed to move boats by hauling on the warps (the ropes attached to the boats)
- **WARRENER:** A person in-charge of a portion of land used for breeding rabbits and other small game.
- **WASHMAN:** A tin coater.
- **WASTEMAN:** A person employed in the mines to check the old workings for gas and maintaining them in good order. A person employed to remove waste.
- **WATCH FINISHER:** A person employed to assemble watches and clocks.
- **WATCHMAN:** A town official who guards the streets at night.
- **WATER BAILIFF:** An official in-charge of the fishing rights on a stretch of water. A river policeman or in coastal towns, a customs official.
- **WATER CARRIER:** A person who carts and sells fresh water.
- **WATER GILDER:** A person who trapped water fowl.
- **WATER LEADER or LEDER or LODER:** A person who transports and sells fresh drinking water.
- **WATERMAN:** A person who works with or on boats usually on rivers.
- **WATTLE HURDLE MAKER:** A person who makes a type of fence from wattle to keep the sheep in.

- WAULKMILLER: A weaver.
- WAY MAN: A surveyor of roads.
- WAY-MAKER: A person employed to make roads.
- WEATHERSPY: An astrologer.
- WEBBER: A weaver.
- WEBSTER: A weaver operating weaving looms (originally a female weaver).
- WEEDER: A person employed to remove the weeds from the gardens of the rich.
- WEIGHER: A person employed on the docks to weigh the cargo as it was unloaded.
- WELL SINKER: A person who digs wells.
- WELL WRIGHT: A person who makes the winding equipment used to raise the bucket in the well.
- WELLMASTER: A person in charge of the local well with the responsibility of ensuring clean water for the village.
- WET GLOVER: A person who makes leather gloves.
- WET NURSE: A woman employed to suckle the child of another (common practice with the rich).
- WETTER: [1] A person employed to dampen paper during the printing process. [2] A person in the glass industry who detaches the glass by wetting.
- WHACKER: A horse or oxen team driver.
- WHARFINGER: A person who owns or is in charge of a wharf.
- WHEELER: A wheel maker, a person in the textile industry who attends to the spinning

wheel, a person who leads the pit ponies that pull the tubs underground in the mines.
- WHEELWRIGHT: A maker or repairer of wagon wheels
- WHEERYMAN: A person in charge of a wheery, a small light rowing boat.
- WHIG: A horse driver (Scottish term).
- WHIPCORD MAKER: A person who makes whips.
- WHIPMAKER: A person who makes whips.
- WHIPPERIN: A person who manages the hounds in a hunt.
- WHIT COOPER: A person who makes barrels, etc from tin.
- WHITE LIMER: A person who plasters walls using lime and water plaster.
- WHITE SMITH: A tin smith.
- WHITEAR: A person who cleans hides.
- WHITENER: A person who bleaches cloth.
- WHITENING ROLL MAKER: A person who makes the whitening used in whitening walls of cottages.
- WHITESMITH: A tinsmith.
- WHITESTER: A person who bleaches cloth.
- WHITEWING: A streetsweeper.
- WHITTAWER: [1] A person who makes saddles and harnesses. [2] A preparer of white leather.
- WILLEYER: A person who throws handfulls of wool or hair, hemp or flax tow, etc., on to brattice or other feed apparatus of willeying machine, which separates fibres, and breaks up their natural matted state, and shakes

out dirt and foreign matter therefrom, in preparation for carding; sometimes also blends materials together in process of willeying.
- WILLOW PLAITER or WEAVER: A person who makes baskets, etc.
- WINDER: In the textile industry, a person who transfers the yarn from bobbins on to cheeses or into balls ready for weaving. In the mines, a person who operates the pulley or winch.
- WINDSTER: A silk winder.
- WIRE DRAWER: A person who makes wire from metal by drawing the metal through various size holes in a template.
- WOODBREAKER: A person who makes wooden water casks.
- WOODRANGER: A person in charge of the forest or woods.
- WOODREEVE: A person in charge of the forest or woods.
- WOODWARD: A person in charge of the forest or woods.
- WOOL DRIVER: A person who brings the wool to market.
- WOOL FACTOR: A wool merchants agent.
- WOOL GROWER: A sheep farmer.
- WOOL MAN: A person who sorts the wool into different grades.
- WOOL STAPLER: A person who sorts the wool into different grades.
- WOOL WINDER: A person who makes up balls of wool for selling.

- **WOOLCOMBER**: A person employed in the woollen mills to operate the machines that separate the fibres ready for spinning.
- **WOOLEN BILLY PIECER**: A person employed in the woollen mills to piece together the broken yarns.
- **WOOLSORTER**: A person who sorts the wool into different grades.
- **WOOLSTED MAN**: From worsted man, a seller of woollen cloth.
- **WORSTED MANUFACTURER**: A person who makes worsted cloth.
- **WORSTED SHEARMAN**: A person who made worsted cloth.
- **WRIGHT**: A skilled worker, builder or repairer in various trades.
- **WRITER**: A person employed to write. A scribe. A clerk etc.
- **WYRTHA**: A labourer.

X

- **XYLOGRAPHER**: A person who uses and makes wooden blocks used in printing illustrations.

Y

- **YARDMAN**: [1] A railroad yard worker, [2] A farm worker.
- **YATMAN**: A gate keeper.
- **YEARMAN**: A person contracted to work for a year.

- **YEOMAN:** [1] A freeholder, the next class down from gentry. [2] An assistant to an official. [3] A ships officer in charge of stores.

Z

- **ZINCOGRAPHER:** A designer who etches in relief a pattern on zinc plates used for printing.
- **ZITHERIST:** A player of a simple, flat many-stringed instrument.
- **ZOETROPE MAKER:** A craftsman who makes zoetropes, an optical toy in the form of a cylinder with a series of pictures painted on the inner surface which gives the impression of continuous motion when viewed through slits in the rotating cylinder.
- **ZOOGRAPHER:** A person who describes and classifies animals.

TYPES OF GOVERNMENTS

democracy	government of, by and for the people
autocracy	government under sovereignty of an individual
aristocracy	government by nobles
bureaucracy	government by officials
oligarchy	government by few
plutocracy	government by the rich

hagiacracy (hagiocracy)	government by priests
gerontocracy	government by old men
dulocracy	government by slaves
endarchy	centralised government
episcopacy	government of the church by bishops
statocracy	government by military class
kakistocracy	government by the worst citizens
autonomy	the right of self-government
referendum	to decide by the direct vote
consort	the wife or husband of a king or queen

Words Denoting Places

Aviary	place where birds are kept
Apiary	bees are kept
Aquarium	fish are kept
Hutch	rabbits are kept
Insectarium	insects are kept
Sty	pigs are kept
Kennel	dogs are kept

Stable	horses are kept
Pen, byre	cows are kept
Dovecot	pigeons and doves are kept
Burrow	animals underground home
Den	home of a lion
Drey	a squirrel's home
Lair	resting place of wild animals
Form	house or bed of a hare
Eyrie, aerie	a nest of a bird of prey
Abattoir	animals are slaughtered for the market
Hangar	place where aeroplanes are housed
Galley, caboose	kitchen of a ship
Archives	place where old records are preserved
Incinerator	place where house refuse is reduced to ashes
Cache	a place where ammunition is hidden
Depot	goods are stored
Garret	room immediately below the roof
Mint	place where money is coined
Quadrangle	square courtyard bounded by walls

Avenue	a broad road lined with trees
Cul-de-sac	a blind alley
Resort	a place frequented for health and pleasure
Refectory	refreshment hall in monastries and convents
Caddy	small box in which tea is kept
Reticule	a lady's handbag or work bag
Cruet	a small bottle to keep sauce

METAPHORS

Some of these metaphors are in common use in English

A ray of hope	A flash of inspiration
The fire of passion	A flow of words
The depths of despair	The dawn of history
The heights of happiness	To bombard with questions
The school of life	To be consumed with curiosity
The wind of change	To overflow with ideas
The book of nature	To strike a note

The key to the mystery	To put up a good fight
The heart of the matter	To burst into tears
The root of the trouble	The crux of the problem

Graphy Words

Graphy comes from 'Graphian' which means to write

bibliography	books
cartography	maps
anthography	flowers
geography	earth
anemography	wind
cryptography	codes
ethnography	people
hydrography	water
orography	mountains
topography	localities
choreography	dancing
calligraphy	handwriting
typography	printing
phonography	sound
electrocardiography	heart

radiography	X-rays
orthography	spelling
lithography	stones

Phile Words

Words pertaining to the love of something.

acrophile	a lover of mountains
aerophilatelist	one who collects air-mail stamps
anglophile	a lover of England and/or the English
bibliophile	a lover of books
cartophily	the collecting of cigarette cards
cumyxaphily	the collecting of match-boxes
discophily	the collecting of gramophone records
hippophile	a lover of horses
peridromophily	the collecting of bus and railway tickets
philanthrope	a lover of mankind
stegophily	a lover of climbing buildings
zoophilist	a lover of animals

Miso Words

Words pertaining to the hate of something.

misanthrope	a hater of mankind
misocapnik	one who hates cigarette smoking
misogamist	one who hates marriage
misogynist	a person who hates women
misologist	one who hates learning or knowledge

Mania Words

An obsession to do something.

anthomania	a great lover of flowers
bibliokleptomania	a mental aberration leading to the stealing of books
dipsomania	the compulsion to drink alcohol
pyromania	the compulsion to start fires

OTHERS

aesthetics	relating to the study or appreciation of beauty.
aficionado	a keen follower of a sport, specially of bullfighting in Spain
alopecia	baldness
amnesia	loss of memory
anorexia	loss of appetite
capnomancy	divination from smoke
cartomancy	divination from playing cards
cheironomy	the science of expression by means of gestures
dyslexia	word blindness
misandry	a morbid fear of men by women
phonocamptics	the study of echoes
pyrotechnics	fireworks
rhabdomancy	divination by rods (dowsing)
serendipity	an aptitude for making fortunate discoveries accidentally
syndrome	a set of symptoms

Ologies

These are some of the important 'Study Words'.

anemology	the science of the winds
arachnology	the study of spiders
campanology	the study of bells and bell ringing
conchology	the science of shells
coprology	obscenity in art and literature
deltiology	the collecting of picture postcards
dendrochronology	the dating by growth of annual rings in trees
eschatology	the doctrine of death and after-life
etymology	the study of the origin and history of words
hagiology	the study of saints
herpetology	the study of reptiles
gerontology	the study of old age
geology	the study of rocks and soil
limnology	the study of lakes or of pond life
nelittology	the study of bees

numismatology	the collecting of coins
ornithology	the study of birds
oology	the study of eggs
orology	the study of mountains
philology	the study of languages
pneumatology	the study of spiritual beings or phenomena
psephology	the scientific study of political elections
scatology	the study of pornographic literature
speleology	the study of caves
tegestology	the collecting and study of beer mats
vulcanology	the study of volcanoes

Literary Words

ledger	a book of accounts showing debits and credits
encyclopedia	a book containing information on all branches of knowledge
bibliography	a list of books
glossary	a list of explanations of rare, technical or obsolete words

memoirs	a written account usually in book form of the interesting and memorable experiences of one's life
watermark	the trademark of the maker seen on paper when it is held up to the light
wiseacre	one who pretends to have a great deal of knowledge
excerpt	an extract of selection from a book of writing
caption	the heading of an article or chapter of a book
jargon	language which is confused and unintelligible
manifesto	a declaration of plans and promises
expurgate	to remove the offensive portions of a book
frontispiece	a picture facing the title page of a book
copyright	the exclusive right of an author or his heirs to publish and sell copies of his writings
erratum	an error or misprint in printing or writing
facsimile	an exact copy of handwriting, printing or of a picture

prologue	a short speech by a player at the beginning of a play
epilogue	a short speech by a player at the end of a play
plagiarism	literary theft
eulogy	a writing or speech in praise of a person
dirge	a mournful song for the dead
soliloquy	speaking to oneself
alliteration	a succession of the same initial letters in a passage
peroration	a concluding part of a speech
harangue	a noisy or vehement speech
hackneyed	language that is very much used

Itis

This is the 'itis' know-how of medicine.

otisis	ear	dermatitis	skin
neuritis	nerves	arthritis	joints
carditis	heart	conjunctivitis	eye
bronchitis	lungs	cystitis	bladder
nephritis	kidneys	tonsillitis	throat

colotis	intestines	meningitis	brain
rhinitis	nose	osteomyelitis	bones
gastritis	stomach	thrombophlebitis	blood vessels
hepatitis	liver	peritonitis	abdomen
myelitis	spine		

Types of People

Fastidious	a person difficult to please
Callous	a person having no sympathy
Credulous	a person who easily believes
Gullible	a person who can easily be cheated
Fatalist	one who believes in fate
Feminist	one who believes in offering equal opportunity to women in every sphere
Teetotaller	one who abstains from alcohol
Fanatic	a person who is wild and extravagant in opinion, particulary in religious matters
Stoic	a person indifferent to pleasure and pain
Epicurist	one devoted to pleasure of eating and drinking

Sadist	a person who derives pleasure from inflicting or watching cruelty
Introvert	a person given to withdrawing from others
Extrovert	a person not given to introspection
Ambivert	a person having both the qualities of an introvert and an extrovert
Pessimist	one who looks on the dark side of things
Optimist	one who looks on the bright side of things
Polyglot	one who understands many languages
Atheist	one who does not believe in the existence of God
Agnostic	one who doubts the existence of God
Egotist	one who delights to speak about himself or thinks only of his own welfare
Altruist	one who devotes his life to the welfare and interest of other people
Dipsomaniac	one who has an irresistible desire for alcoholic drinks
Misocapnic	one who hates cigarette smoking

Misanthrope	one who hates mankind
Philanthropist	one who devotes his service or wealth for the love of mankind
Somnambulist	one who walks in his sleep
Somniloquist	one who talks in his sleep
Ventriloquist	one who has the art of speaking in such a way that the sound seems to come from another person
Ambidextrous	a person who can use both his hands equally well
Industrious	a hard working person
Judicious	a sensible and prudent person
Fugitive	one who runs away from the law
Alien	one who takes refuge in a foreign land
Kleptomaniac	one who has an irresistible tendency to steal
Biblioklept	one who steals books
Iconoclast	one who breaks images or church ornaments
Martyr	one who dies for a noble cause
Recluse, hermit	one who leads a solitary life
Conscript	one who is compelled by law to serve as a soldier

Novice	one new to anything
Zoophilist	a lover of animals
Amateur	one who engages in any pursuit for the love of it and not for gain
Frutarian	one who feeds on fruits
Cannibal	one who feeds on human flesh
Itinerant	one who travels from place to place
Mendicant	one who begs for alms
Connoisseur	a critical judge of art and taste
Raconteur	an expert at telling stories
Eavesdropper	one who quietly listens to other peoples conversations
Mountebank	one who pretends to know a great deal about everything
Mimic	imitates the voice and gestures of others
Chaperon	one who accompanies as a guard to a young lady
Numismatist	one who collects coins
Obscurant	one who is opposed to intellectual progress
Pantophagist	one who eats all kinds of food
Blonde	a woman with light coloured hair
Brunette	a woman with dark hair

Coiffeur	a person who dresses up women's hair
Termagant	a noisy and abusive woman

COMMON MEDICAL TERMS

Epidemic	a disease affecting at the same place and time
Endemic	a disease confined to a particular district or place
Sporadic	a disease affecting widely scattered groups of people
Antiseptic	a substance which destroys or awakens germs
Anaesthetic	any medicine which produces insensibility
Anodyne	a medicine which alleviates pain
Cicatrice	the mark or scar left after a wound is healed
Antidote	a medicine to counteract poison
Immune	free or exempt from infection
Emetic	a medicine to cause vomiting
Quarantine	confinement to one place to avoid spread of infection
Amputate	to cut off a part of a person's body which is infected

Panacea	a cure for all diseases
Convalescent	one who is recovering from illness
Convalescence	gradual recovery from illness
Anaemia	want of blood
Deodorant	a substance to keep off bad smells
Fumigate	to disinfect by smoke

MORE WORDS CONFUSED

Word 1	Meaning	Word 2	Meaning
Advice	recommendations about what to do	Advise	to recommend something
Affect	to change or make a difference to	Effect	a result; to bring about a result
Aisle	a passage between rows of seats	Isle	an island
All together	all in one place, all at once	Altogether	completely; on the whole
Along	moving or extending horizontally on	A long	referring to something of great length

Word 1	Meaning	Word 2	Meaning
Aloud	out loud	Allowed	permitted
Altar	a sacred table in a church	Alter	to change
Amoral	not concerned with right or wrong	Immoral	not following accepted moral standards
Appraise	to assess	Apprise	to inform someone
Assent	agreement, approval	Ascent	the action of rising or climbing up
Aural	relating to the ears or hearing	Oral	relating to the mouth; spoken
Balmy	pleasantly warm	Barmy	foolish, crazy
Bare	naked; to uncover	Bear	to carry; to put up with
Bated	in phrase 'with bated breath', i.e. in great suspense	Baited	with bait attached or inserted
Bazaar	a Middle Eastern market	Bizarre	strange

Word 1	Meaning	Word 2	Meaning
Berth	a bunk in a ship, train, etc.	Birth	the emergence of a baby from the womb
Born	having started life	Borne	carried
Bough	a branch of a tree	Bow	to bend the head; the front of a ship
Brake	a device for stopping a vehicle; to stop a vehicle	Break	to separate into pieces; a pause
Breach	to break through, or break a rule; a gap	Breech	the back part of a gun barrel
Broach	to raise a subject for discussion	Brooch	a piece of jewellery
Canvas	a type of strong cloth	Canvass	to seek people's votes
Censure	to criticise strongly	Censor	to ban parts of a book or film; a person who does this

Word 1	Meaning	Word 2	Meaning
Cereal	a grass producing an edible grain; a breakfast food made from grains	Serial	happening in a series
Chord	a group of musical notes	Cord	a length of string; a cord-like body part
Climactic	forming a climax	Climatic	relating to climate
Coarse	rough	Course	a direction; a school subject; part of a meal
Complacent	smug and self-satisfied	Complaisant	willing to please
Complement	to add to so as to improve; an addition that improves something	Compliment	to praise or express approval; an admiring remark
Council	a group of people who manage or advise	Counsel	advice; to advise

Word 1	Meaning	Word 2	Meaning
Cue	a signal for action; a wooden rod	Queue	a line of people or vehicles
Curb	to keep something in check; a control or limit	Kerb	(in British English) the stone edge of a pavement
Currant	a dried grape	Current	happening now; a flow of water, air, or electricity
Defuse	to make a situation less tense	Diffuse	to spread over a wide area
Desert	a waterless, empty area; to abandon someone	Dessert	the sweet course of a meal
Discreet	careful not to attract attention	Discrete	separate and distinct
Disinterested	impartial	Uninterested	not interested
Draught	a current of air	Draft	a first version of a piece of writing

Word 1	Meaning	Word 2	Meaning
Draw	an even score at the end of a game	Drawer	a sliding storage compartment
Dual	having two parts	Duel	a fight or contest between two people
Elicit	to draw out a reply or reaction	Illicit	not allowed by law or rules
Ensure	to make certain that something will happen	Insure	to provide compensation if a person dies or property is damaged
Envelop	to cover or surround	Envelope	a paper container for a letter
Exercise	physical activity; to do physical activity	Exorcise	to drive out an evil spirit
Fawn	a young deer; light brown	Faun	a mythical being, part man, part goat

Word 1	Meaning	Word 2	Meaning
Flaunt	to display ostentatiously	Flout	to disregard a rule
Flounder	to move clumsily; to have difficulty doing something	Founder	to fail
Forbear	to refrain	Forebear	an ancestor
Foreword	an introduction to a book	Forward	onwards, ahead
Freeze	to turn to ice	Frieze	a decoration along a wall
Grisly	gruesome, revolting	Grizzly	a type of bear
Hoard	a store	Horde	a large crowd of people
Imply	to suggest indirectly	Infer	to draw a conclusion
Loath	reluctant, unwilling	Loathe	to hate
Loose	to unfasten; to set free	Lose	to be deprived of; to be unable to find

Word 1	Meaning	Word 2	Meaning
Meter	a measuring device	Metre	a metric unit; rhythm in verse
Militate	to be a powerful factor against	Mitigate	to make less severe
Palate	the roof of the mouth	Palette	a board for mixing colours
Pedal	a foot-operated lever	Peddle	to sell goods
Pole	a long, slender piece of wood	Poll	voting in an election
Pour	to flow or cause to flow	Pore	a tiny opening; to study something closely
Practice	the use of an idea or method; the work or business of a doctor, dentist, etc.	Practice	to do something repeatedly to gain skill; to do something regularly
Prescribe	to authorise use of medicine; to order authoritatively	Proscribe	to officially forbid something

Word 1	Meaning	Word 2	Meaning
Principal	most important; the head of a school	Principle	a fundamental rule or belief
Sceptic	a person inclined to doubt	Septic	infected with bacteria
Sight	the ability to see	Site	a location
Stationary	not moving	Stationery	writing materials
Storey	a level of a building	Story	a tale or account
Titillate	to arouse interest	Titivate	to make more attractive
Tortuous	full of twists; complex	Torturous	full of pain or suffering
Wreath	a ring-shaped arrangement of flowers etc.	Wreathe	to surround or encircle

POTPOURRI

- Abash - make ashamed, dispirited
- Abate - beat down, diminish, lessen
- Ad hoc - relating exclusively to the subject in question

- Addendum - something that is added, as in to the back of a book
- Adulterate - to make impure by adding bogus ingredients
- Amatory - pertaining to lovemaking
- Amiable - pleasing, loving, friendly
- Amicable - friendly, peaceful
- Appease - satisfy an appetite or demand
- Apropos - to the purpose, in reference to
- Ardent - fervent in feeling, intense, passionate
- Arduous - wearisome
- Auspice - flavouring influence; protection, a favourable circumstance
- Axiom - universal proposition; easily proved
- Calamity - disaster, a great misfortune
- Candour - sincerity (I appreciate your candour)
- Canny - wary, prudent
- Cantankerous - perverse in disposition, ill-natured
- Caveat - a warning, let the buyer beware
- Compunction - slight regret or prick of conscience
- Confabulate - converse
- Conjugate - formed in a pair, coupled; inflection of verbs
- Consortium - society, association
- Conundrum - riddle or hard question
- Copious - abundant, plentiful
- Coquette - a flirt
- Cursory - hasty and superficial a glance
- Daunting - intimidating, discouraging

- Debase - same as adulterate
- Decorous - well-behaved, proper
- Decorum - the standards of conduct approved by society, propriety
- Deference - submission to the judgement of another, respectful
- Defunct - dead
- Demeanor - behaviour
- Demitasse - small cup of black coffee
- Deplorable - lamentable, calamitous
- Diabolic - devilish. (diabolical)
- Diminutive - very small or tiny, a small thing or person
- Disparage - discredit
- Disparity - essentially different, unequal
- Effigy - a life size dummy or sculpture of a person
- Effrontery - barefaced, impropriety, impudence
- Eminent - high in rank, office, worth; conspicuous, noteworthy
- Enamored - inflame with love, captivate
- Esoteric - understood by a select few secret; mysterious
- Exorbitant - excessive, inordinate, going beyond usual or proper bounds
- Extenuate - make smaller in degree of appearance
- Extrapolate - project on the basis of known data; surmise
- Fastidious - hard to please, over nice
- Fetid - having an offensive stench

- Fortuitous - coming by chance, accidental
- Frivolous - not seriously intended, trivial or silly
- Fusiform - spindle shaped, i.e. streamlined.
- Gad - ramble about idly
- Gallivant - seek pleasure frivolously; gad about
- Gam - school of whales
- Gambit - any apparent sacrifice in expectation of later gain
- Germane - closely allied, relevant
- Goad - to urge
- Guile - cunning
- Imminent - likely to occur soon; impending
- Impeccable - without fault or blemish, perfect
- Impecunious - without money, poor
- Impetuous - impulse, incentive
- Impious - profane, disrespectful, impiety
- Impudence - gall, offensively forward in behaviour, insolent, saucy
- Incessant - continuing without interruption
- Inexorable - not to be persuaded or moved
- Infallible - free from fallacy, trustworthy
- Infirm - not in good health
- Inflammatory - serving to inflame, excite highly, make violent, aggravate
- Inflect - turn from a direct course; bend
- Ingenuous - candid naive, free from guile (gile)
- Innate - existing in one from birth
- Innocuous - harmless
- Inoculate - inject an immunising agent into

- Insipid - dull, flavourless
- Interim - an intervening time, the meantime
- Inundate - flood, deluge, overwhelm
- Iridescent - glittering with changeable colours like a rainbow
- Ironclad - armoured
- Irreverent - disrespectful
- Jettison - Throw goods overboard to lighten a ship
- Judicious - exercising sound judgement; prudent
- Kudos - praise, glory
- Lambasting - whacking or pounding
- Lexicon - a dictionary, special vocabulary
- Macabre - gruesome, dance of death
- Myopic - near sightedness
- Myrmidon - one who obeys or follows without question or scruple
- Nebulous - cloudy, hazy, confused
- Oblique - slanting, indirectly aimed or expressed
- Obsequious - fawning, servile, deferential
- Opaque - cloudy
- Ornery - of ugly disposition, hard to manage
- Paleolithic - pertaining to old stone age
- Paradigm - a list of the inflected forms of a word
- Parnassus - a centre of or inspiration for poetic or artistic work
- Percipient - perceiving
- Permutation - any possible arrangement of any units in a group
- Pernicious - Highly destructive

- Perplexity - problem, puzzled, make confused
- Persecute - harass, make suffer for divergent principles
- Persnickety - excessively meticulous
- Peruse - read attentively. (a quick perusal)
- Preamble - a preface, opening remarks
- Precarious - uncertain, insecure
- Preclude - impede, prevent
- Predisposition - innate tendency
- Propriety - fitness, rightness, correct behaviour, decorum
- Prosaic - unromantic, commonplace
- Protean - readily assuming many shapes
- Protege - a person protected or aided by another
- Protuberant - bulging out; prominent
- Proverbial - well-known
- Pukka - genuine, first rate
- Pulchritude – beauty
- Quagmire - area of muddy ground, marsh difficult position or situation
- Qualm - twinge of conscience
- Quarrel - dispute
- Quasi - seemingly or almost, not wholly genuine
- Regalia - emblems, insignia or personal finery
- Regimental - being under strict and uniform control
- Relegate - send away or out of the way, consign, relegation
- Reticent - silent or reserved
- Reverent - respectful; devout

- Sagacious - wise, sagacity
- Sanctum - a private retreat (sanctumoneous)
- Sans - without
- Sequester - put aside (sequestered)
- Simpatico - congenial
- Smug - self-satisfied
- Specious - apparently, deceptive
- Sybarite - a self-indulgent, luxury loving person
- Sycophant - a servile flatterer
- Syllabus - compendium, an abstract
- Symbiotic - living together of two different Species harmoniously
- Tenacious - persistant in an opinion or view, stubborn
- Tenure - The holding of something, as in property, office, etc.
- Transpire - emit, exhale or perspire, happen occur
- Tumultuous - violently disturbing, highly exciting
- Ubiquitous - existing everywhere
- Umbrage - resentment
- Uncanny - weird
- Verbose - wordy

| And More |

Words Easily Confused

1. Accept (to receive)
   Except (to exclude. Also a preposition)

2. Adverse (hostile)
   Averse (marks an actual sentiment of dislike, disinclines)
3. Application (to apply for some favour, leave, etc.)
   Implication (that which is involved, implied)
4. Assent (to agree)
   Ascent (climb)
5. Allusion (reference)
   Illusion (deception)
6. Apposite (suitable)
   Opposite (contrary)
7. Ascetic (one who devotes himself to a life of solitude and contemplation, with the rigorous discipline of self)
   Ascetic (artistic, pertaining to beauty for instance, a person of aesthetic sensibilities)
8. Attenuate (to make thin)
   Extenuate (to diminish, lessen, excuse, e.g. extenuating circumstances)
9. Avert (to ward off)
   Invert (to turn upside down)
10. Bridal (belonging to a bride or wedding)
    Bridle (horse's reins)
11. Beside (almost always a preposition, meaning "by the side of")
    Besides (often an adverb, signifying "in addition")
12. Beneficial (useful)
    Beneficent (doing good)
    Benevolent (charitable, wishing well)

13. Canvas (a coarse cloth used for painting, sails or tents)
    Canvass (to solicit votes)
14. Cast (to throw)
    Caste (sect or community)
15. Confirm (to ratify)
    Conform (to agree with or subscribe to rules or principles
16. Collision (conflict, a violent meeting)
    Collusion (a secret agreement for a deceitful purpose)
17. Comity (courtesy as between equals)
    Committee (a group of persons)
18. Contagious (infectious)
    Contiguous (adjoining, near)
19. Decease (death)
    Disease (illness, malady)
20. Duel (a combat between two persons)
    Dual (two-fold-of dual significance)
21. Excess (that which goes beyond normal limit)
    Access (the privilege or right to come or approach someone)
22. Excite (is said more particularly of the inner feelings- to stir, to rouse)
    Incite (is said of the external action- to incite someone to violence)
23. Factious (disloyal or turbulent)
    Fictitious (unreal, imaginary)
24. Graceful (full of grace, comely, beautiful)
    Gracious (full of kindness, e.g. your gracious self)

25. Hail (to greet someone from a distance, or frzen rain)
    Hale (healthy)
26. Imaginary (unreal)
    Imagination (the faculty of forming images in the mind)
27. Ingenuous (open and frank)
    Ingenious (clever or skilful)
28. Judicious (possessing sound judgement, discreet)
    Judicial (pertaining to a judge, or a court of justice)
29. Metal (gold, silver etc.)
    Mettle (spirit or courage)
30. Momentous (historic, significant)
    Momentary (short-lived, transient)
31. Odious (contemptible)
    Odorous (sweet-smelling, fragrant)
32. Pursued (followed)
    Persuade (to convince)
33. Personal (pertaining to an individual, e.g. this is my personal file)
    Personnel (Body of persons employed in any service)
34. Query (question)
    Quarry (object of pursuit by bird of prey, hounds, hunters etc.)
35. Remisses (negligence of duty)
    Remission (forgiveness of sins)
36. Strait (narrow)
    Straight (direct)

37. Taut (stretched or tight)
    Taught (educated or tight)
38. Teem (to be full of, e.g. a river teeming with fish)
    Team (a group or set of players- for hockey, cricket, football, etc.)
39. Tear (liquid falling from the eye)
    Tier (a row or rank)
40. Truth (something true)
    Truism (something obvious, trite, common place)
41. Vein (a blood artery)
    Vain (conceited, proud)
    Vane (weather cock)
42. Veil (a curtain)
    Wail (to bemoan, to be full of sorrow)
43. Virtuous (full of virtue, goodness)
    Virtual (actual, real)
44. Wave (ripples on the surface of the water)
    Waive (to give up claim to something)
45. Wet (moist)
    Whet (to sharpen)

Greek Words

Along with Latin, Greek is probably the language that most influenced other languages around the world. Many English words derive directly from Greek ones, and knowing their origin and meaning is important.

Here are 12 Greek words that are commonly used in our society. The next time you hear someone saying "Kudos to you," you will know where it comes from.

Acme	The highest point of a structure.
Acropolis	Acro means edge or extremity, while polis means city. Acropolis, therefore, refers to cities that were built with security purposes in mind.
Agora	The Agora was an open market place, present in most cities of the ancient Greece. Today, the term can be used to express any type of open assembly or congregation.
Anathema	Anathema is a noun and it means a formal ban, curse or excommunication.
Anaemia	Anaemia refers to a condition characterised by a qualitative or quantitative deficiency of the red blood cells (or of the haemoglobin).
Ethos	Translated literally from the Greek, ethos means "accustomed place." It refers to a disposition or characteristics peculiar to a specific person, culture or movement.
Dogma	Dogma refers to the established belief or set of principles held by a religion, ideology or by any organisation. Dogmas are also authoritative and undisputed. Outside of the religious context, therefore, the term tends to carry a negative connotation.

Eureka	The exclamation Eureka is used to celebrate a discovery, and it can be translated to "I have found!". It is attributed to the famous Greek mathematician Archimedes.
Genesis	Genesis means birth or origin. Genesis is also the name of the first book of the Bible.
Phobia	Many people wrongly think that a phobia is a fear. In reality it is more than that. Phobia is an irrational and exaggerated fear of something. The fear can be associated with certain activities, situations, things or people.
Plethora	You have a plethora when you go beyond what is needed or appropriate. It represents an excess or undesired abundance.
Kudos	Kudos means fame or glory, usually resulting from an important act or achievement.

Food & Cooking Words

Bake	Cook by dry heat in an oven
Batter	A mixture of flour mixed with water or milk. It should be thin enough to pour
Blanch	To remove the skins of vegetables or fruits by dipping them in boiling water

Blend	To mix two or more ingredients together thoroughly
Brush	Spread thinly
Chill	To allow to become very cold but not frozen
Chop	To cut meat or vegetables into small pieces with a knife
Cream together	To mix two or more ingredients together till smooth and creamy
Deep fry	To cook in hot oil in a deep pan so that the food floats in the oil while frying
Dissolve	To cause the ingredient to merge completely in the liquid it is mixed in
Dust	To coat lightly with flour
Fold in	To mix in new ingredients gently
Garnish	To decorate
Grate	To shred fruits or vegetables into tiny pieces by rubbing against a grater
Knead	To mix dough with the hands by pressing and folding
Mince	To cut into very small pieces e.g. meat, nuts etc.
Marinate	To soak meat or vegetables completely with other ingredients and let it stand for a few hours to become tender
Peel	To remove the outer skin of fruits or vegetables

Roll out	To spread out and flatten dough with a rolling pin
Shred	To cut into thin long pieces
Shallow fry	To cook in a very small quantity of oil in a flat pan
Sift	To pass through a sieve to remove coarser particles
Simmer	To cook on very low heat below the boiling point
Soak	To immerse in liquid for sometime
Stir	To mix with a spoon using circular motion
Whip	To beat rapidly
A dash of liquid	A few drops
Boil	Liquid produces bubbles over high fire.
Braise	To cook food, usually meat or vegetables over a long period of time. Food undergoes searing (see sear) before it's braised
Dice	Cut into small even pieces
Dry-fry	No oil is used when frying, e.g. chill or curry paste
Grill	To cook food usually over hot coals. Popular cooking method for steaks, chicken wings, hamburgers and salmon
Julienne	It's a French word that simply means to cut food into very thin strips

Marinate	Seasonings are rubbed on to meat, fish and vegetables to create better taste. Marinated food is often set aside for 15 minutes or a couple of hours or even left overnight
Minced	Chopped till very fine
Poach	To cook in liquid heated over a low fire
Roast	To cook meat in an oven
Sauté	A French word that refers to cooking food quickly over medium to high fire with little oil. Tossing is needed to prevent over-browning
Sear	Where meat is subjected to high fire for browning to take place in order to seal in the meat juices. It causes meat to be soft and tender. However, meat at this point may not be fully cooked
Stock	A strained solution obtained after boiling water with added ingredients such as pork, chicken or fish bones, shells from shellfish (e.g. shrimps, clams and abalone) or other seasonings
Steam	To cook using steam from boiling water. Make sure the water in the steamer/wok is boiling before cooking the food
Stew	To cook either by boiling or simmering in a tightly covered pot over a long period of time

Stir-fry	To fry small pieces (such as garlic and onions) over high fire

Portmanteau Words

A word formed by merging the sounds and meanings of two different words, portmanteau words are also called Centaur Words.

Absatively	absolutely + positively
Adflation	advertising + inflation
Beautility	beauty + utility
Bit	binary + digit
Bitini	bitsy + bikini
Blog	web + log
Bonk	bang + conk
Breathalyzer	breath + analyzer
Brunch	breakfast + lunch
Camcorder	camera + recorder
Chortle	chuckle + snort
Cremains	cremated + remains
Chunnel	channel + tunnel
Diplonomics	diplomacy + economics
E-commerce	electronic + commerce
Email	electronic + mail
Faction	fact + fiction

Fantabulous	fantastic + fabulous
Fanzine	fanatic + magazine
Feminar	feminine + seminar
Frarority	fraternity + sorority
Gasohol	gasoline + alcohol
Ginormous	gigantic + enormous
Guestimate	guess + estimate
Hi-tech	high + technology
Heliport	helicopter + airport
Internet	international + network
Interpol	international + police
Advertainment	advertisement + entertainment
Advertorial	advertisement + editorial
Affluenza	affluence + influenza
Because	by + cause
Bionic	biology + electronic
Brunch	breakfast + lunch
Cellophane	cellulose + diaphane
Chillaxing	chilling + relaxing
Chingilish	Chinese + English
Cineplex	cinema + complex
Diabesity	diabetes + obesity
Dumbfound	dumb + comfound

Econocrat	economist + bureaucrat
Edutainment	education + entertainment
Fortnight	fourteen + nights
Franglish	French + English
Freeware	free + software
Gainsay	against + say
Globish	global + English
Glitz	glamour + ritz
Goodbye	God + be(with) + ye
Hassle	haggle + tussle
Hinglish	Hindi + English
Infomercial	information + communication
Infotainment	information + entertainment
Intercom	internal + communication
Internet	international + network
Japlish	Japanese + English
Knowledgebase	knowledge + database
Lox	liquid + oxygen
Moblog	mobile + weblog
Modem	modulator + demodulator
Motel	motor + hotel
Motorcade	motor + cavalcade
Multiplex	multiple + complex

Netiquette	internet + etiquette
Seascape	sea + landscape
Sitcom	situation + comedy
Smaze	smoke
Smog	smoke + fog
Soundscape	sound + landscape
Stagflation	stagnation + inflation
Telegenic	television + photogenic
Telex	teleprinter + monologue
Travelogue	travel + monologue
Tween	teen + between
Webinar	web + seminar
WiFi	Wireless + fidelity
Zonkey	Zebra + donkey

SYNONYMS

Synonyms are words of approximately the same meaning

abnormal	unusual, exceptional, odd, peculiar
abridge	shorten, curtail, condense
abundant	plentiful, copious, ample
accumulate	collect, acquire, get together, build up

acquiesce	agree, assent, consent, concur
arduous	hard, difficult, strenuous
brusque	blunt, off-hand, sharp
competent	qualified, able, effective
conspicuous	outstanding, obvious, striking
covetous	envious, greedy
deceive	cheat, mislead, misrepresent, lie
depose	removed, unseat, demote
detest	hat, loathe, abominate
discord	strife, quarrel, disagreement
eminent	distinguished, notable, outstanding
exquisite	delicate, fine, keen (of pleasure)
festive	joyous, jovial, happy
genial	friendly, warm, kindly
hazardous	dangerous, risky, reckless
impudent	cheeky, pert, shameless
inception	start, beginning
irate	angry, annoyed, furious
jubilant	joyful, delighted
knavery	dishonesty, roguery, wickedness
lament	sorrow, grief, elegy

languid	feeble, faint, dropping
manifest	show, demonstrate, reveal
meager	scarce, thin, scanty, insufficient
miniature	small, diminutive, tiny
notable	important, famous, known
odium	hate, dislike, loathing
potent	strong, powerful, cogent, influential
prudent	wise, careful, discreet
quench	slake (thirst), extinguish, stifle
querulous	complaining, peevish, dissatisfied
recompense	reward, requite, compensate
refresh	re-animate, re-invigorate, restore
refuge	shelter, haven
slender	thin, slim, scanty
staid	quiet, sober, withdrawn
urge	exhort, press, entreat
vivacious	lively, bright, cheerful
waver	vacillate, hesitate, change (opinion)
wretched	unhappy, miserable, poor

Antonyms

Pairs of words having opposite or contrary meanings are called antonyms.

absolute	limited, relative	condemn	approve
accept	refuse	confess	deny
acknowledge	disown, deny	contract	expand
acquit	convict	credit	cash, debit
acute	obtuse	difficult	easy
adversity	prosperity	diligent	idle
affirm	deny	diminish	increase
affluence	poverty	discount	premium
agree	differ	docile	stubborn
attack	defend	economical	extravagant
attract	repel	elevation	depression
barbarous	civilised	encourage	discourage
base	noble	endless	finite
benevolence	malevolence	enrich	impoverish

blunt	sharp	enthusiasm	apathy, indifference
bold	timid	exterior	interior
bright	dull	extravagant	frugal
broad	narrow	fact	fiction
care	neglect	fade	bloom
careful	careless	falsehood	truth
compliance	refusal	fickle	constant
fruitful	barren	frank	reserved
gain	loss	particular	general
genuine	spurious	peace	war
happiness	misery	permanent	temporary
haste	delay	pleasant	dull
honour	shame	prohibit	permit
hope	despair	real	fictitious
humble	haughty, proud	reject	accept
intentional	accidental	repulsive	attractive
keen	dull	smooth	rugged, rough

knowledge	ignorance	strange	familiar
lenient	rigorous, severe	sympathy	antipathy
make	mar	uniform	variable
		virtue	vice

DISTINCTIVE NAMES GIVEN TO THE YOUNG OF ANIMALS

cat	kitten	sheep	lamb
cock	cockerel	hen	pullet
cow	calf	cow	heifer
horse	foal	bull	calf
ass	foal	deer	fawn
dog	puppy	mare	filly
pig	piglet	trout	fry
elephant	calf	salmon	parr
whale	calf	bird	nestling
eagle	eaglet	hawk	bowet
owl	owlet	eel	elver
fowl	chicken	lion, bear, fox	cub
goat	kid	swan	cygnet
goose	gosling		

WORDS DENOTING SOUNDS

Animal Sounds

Apes - gibber	Dogs - yelp, bark, whine, growl
Asses - bray	Deer - bell, howl
Bears - growl	Doves - coo
Bees - hum	
Beetles - drone	Ducks - quack
Birds - sing, twitter, chirp	Eagles - scream
Bulls - bellow	Elephants - trumpet
Camels - grunt	Flies - buzz
Cats - mew, purr, caterwaul	Pea - fowl - scream
Cattle - bellow	Pigeons - coo
Cocks - crow	pigs - grunt, squeal
Cows - low	Puppies - yelp
Crickets - chirp	Ravens - croak
Crows - caw	Rooks - caw
Rabbits - squeal	Monkeys - chatter, gibber
Foxes - yelp, bark	Nightingales - sing, warble
Frogs - croak	Owls - hoot, screech, scream
Geese - cackle, gabble, hiss	Oxen - low, bellow

Goats - bleat
Hawks - scream
Hens - cackle, cluck
Horses - neigh, snort, whinny
Hounds - bay
Hyenas - laugh
Jackals - howl
Kittens - mew
Lambs - bleat
Larks - sing, warble
Lions - roar
Magpies - chatter
Mice - squeak

Parrots - talk
Seagulls - scream
Sheep - bleat
Small birds - chirp, twitter, pipe

Snakes - hiss
Swans - cry
Thrushes - whistle
Tigers - growl, roar
Turkeys - gobble
Vultures - scream
Wolves - howl
Wrens - warble

Non - Animal Sounds

Pattering of the rain

Gurling or lapping of the rivers

Babbling of the brooks

Splashing of water

Swashing of the sea

Swishing of ladies' skirts

Whizzing of arrows

Buzzing of a telephone

Zooming of aeroplanes

Cracking of fire, wood, dry leaves

Tinkling of coins

Jingling, chiming of bells

Hooting of a steam whistle	Shuffling of feet
Tooting of a horn	Whirring of wings
Screeching of brakes	Crinkling of paper
Roaring, rolling, rumbling of thunder	Clangour of hammers
Rumbling of heavy vehicles	Clanking of chains
Clatter of horses' hoofs	Ticking of clocks
Creaking of hinges	Crack of a whip
Hissing of steam	Rustle of silk or leaves

Words Pertaining to the Church

Krasis	the mixing of water and wine
Diocese	the district under the jurisdiction of a bishop
Aisle	passage between the pew of a church
Sexton	person incharge of a church building
Offertory	the money given by the congregation at a church service

Ordination	the ceremony when Holy Orders are taken and a man becomes a priest
Crypt	a vault beneath the church used for the burial of the dead
Encyclical	a letter from the Pope of the Roman Catholics all over the world
Vestry	a room attached to the church
Presbytery	the residence of a priest
Chorister	one who sings in the choir
Lectern	a reading desk from where the scriptures are read
Pulpit	the stand from which a preacher delivers his sermon
Crosier	a bishop's staff
Mitre	a bishop's cap
Cassock	loose garment worn by priests
Cope	a cloak - like vestment worn by priests at solemn ceremonies
Chalice	the cup used in the Eucharist
Laity	people distinct from clergy
Synod	a council of clergymen
Font	the vessel containing water for baptism
Dean	the head of a cathedral
Archdeacon	a clergyman in rank after a bishop

Deacon	one in the lowest degree of Holy Orders in the Anglican church		
Aureole	the circle of light seen round the head of Christ and Saints		
Matins	morning service of the Anglican church		
Vespers	evening service		
Apostate	one who renounces his religious vows		
Proselyte	one who is converted from one religion to another		
Acolyte	one who assists at services by lighting candles		
Censer	a vessel for burning incense		
Crusade	the holy war of Christians		
Crescentade	"Jehad" or the holy war of the Muslims		

ADJECTIVES

How often we find ourselves searching for words to describe things and persons! Here are a few.

Goats	Caprine	Ships, sailors	Nautical
Eagle	Aquiline	Ships	Naval
Horses	Equine, Calavine,	Spring	Vernal

Lion	Leonine	Autumn	Autumnal
Hares	Leporine	Mother	Maternal
Wolf	Lupine	Father	Paternal
Peacock	Pavinine	Sister	Sororal
Pigeons	Peristeronic	Brother	Fraternal
Fish	Piscine	Uncle	Avuncular
Parrots	Psittaceous	Duke	Ducal
Fox	Vulpine	Son or daughter	Filial
Swine, pigs	Porcine	Milk	Lacteal
Cats	Feline	Infant	Infantile
Goose	Anserine	Servant	Menial
Shepherds	Pastoral, Bucolic	Sea	Maritime, Marine
Priest	Sacerdotal	Belly	Alvine
Priesthood	Hieratic	Brain	Cerebral
Author	Auctorial	Heart	Cardiac
Tailor	Sartorial	Iron	Ferrous
Barber	Tonsorial	Tin	Stanic
Wife	Uxorial	Silk	Sericate
Day	Diurnal	River	Fluvial
Morning	Matinal	Leaves	Foliar
Evening	Vesper	Rope	Funicular
Night	Nocturnal	Island	Insular
Marriage	Connubial / nuptial	Tears	Lachrymal

Matrimony	Conjugal	Lamp	Lucermal
Love	Erotic	Country	Rural, rustic
Heaven	Celestial	Town, city	Urban
Earth	Terrestrial	Money	Monetary/ Pecuniary/ Fiscal
Cattle	Bovine	Coins	Numismatic
Dogs	Canine	Preaching	Predicatory
Sheep	Ovine	Colour	Chromatic
Crow	Corvine	Kitchen	Culinary
Wild beasts	Ferine	Law court	Forensic
Smelling	Olfactory	Dancing	Terpsichorean
Seeing	Visual / Optical	Weaving	Textiles
Asses	Asinine	Fishing	Piscatory
Hearing	Auditory / aural	First age	Primeval
Bees	Apiarian	Old age	Senile
Sound	Acoustic	Fats	Sebaceous
Air	Pneumatic	Moon	Lunar
Rain	Pluvial	Stars	Stellar

Sun	Solar		Petrine
Land	Praedial	Water	Aquatic
Gums	Gingival		Pauline
Throat	Guttural	Bernard Shaw	Shavian
Lips	Labial		
Hair	Crinal	Tongue	Glossal
Nose	Nasal		
Floods	Diluvial		
Parish	Parochial		
Lungs	Pulmonary	Alps	Alpine

Proverbs

'What oft was thought but ne'er so well expressed.'

- A beggar can never be bankrupt
- A bird in the hand is worth two in the bush
- A burnt child dreads fire
- A cheerful wife is the joy of life
- A drunkard's purse is a bottle
- A fault confessed is half redressed
- A friend is easier lost than found
- A friend's frown is better than a fool's smile
- A good name is sooner lost than found
- A great talker is a great liar
- A hungry man is an angry man

- A man in debt is caught in a net
- A miss is as good as a mile
- A penny saved is a penny gained
- A rolling stone gathers no moss
- A short cut is often a wrong cut
- A stitch in time saves nine
- A thing begun is half done
- A wife, a dog and a walnut tree, the more you beat them the better they will be
- A wise man changes his mind sometimes but a fool never
- Absence makes the heart grow fonder
- Advice when most needed is least heeded
- All's fair in love and war
- An empty bag cannot stand upright
- An idle mind is a devil's workshop
- An old bird is not to be caught with chaff
- Appetite comes with eating
- As you sow, so you shall reap
- Barking dogs seldom bite
- Be just before you are generous
- Better late than never
- Boys will be boys
- By timely mending save much spending
- Cheapest is dearest
- Courtesy costs nothing
- Curses are like chicken, they come home to roost
- Diligence is the best teacher
- Do not cut off your nose to spite your face
- Do not count your chickens before they are hatched

- Do not trouble till trouble troubles you
- Easier said than done
- Eat to live, do not live to eat
- Enough is good as a feast to one who is not a beast
- Every ass likes to hear himself bray
- Every cloud has a silver lining
- Every dog has his day
- Every why has a wherefore
- Everything comes to those who wait
- Example is better than precept
- Experience keeps a dear school but fools will learn in no other
- Familiarity breeds contempt
- First come, first served
- Fools build houses and wise men buy them
- Give a fool rope enough and he will hang himself
- Give and spend and God will send
- Good wine needs no bush
- Great haste makes great waste
- Great minds think alike
- Great talkers are little doers
- Habit is second nature
- Hasty climbers have sudden falls
- He giveth twice who giveth in a trice
- He is richest who has fewest wants
- He knows most who speaks least
- He laughs best who laughs last
- He who will lend will lose a friend
- He that goes a-borrowing goes a-sorrowing
- He that loves glass without "G" takes away "L" and that is he

- He is no man who cannot say "No"
- Hunger is the best sauce
- If a man deceive me once shame on him; if twice shame on me
- Ill got ill –spent
- If you wish for peace, prepare for war
- It is a good horse that never stumbles and a good wife that never grumbles
- It is easier to pull down than to build
- It is folly to pull down than to build
- It is folly to live in Rome and strive with the Pope
- It never rains but it pours
- Kindness begets kindness
- Lazy people take the most pains
- Let bygones be bygones
- Loans and debts make worries and frets
- Lost time is never found
- Make every bargain clear and plain that none should later complain
- Make short the miles with talk and smiles
- Masters two, will not do
- Neither wise men nor fools can work without tools
- Never cross the bridge until you come to it
- Never look a gift horse in the mouth
- Never put off till tomorrow what may be done today
- Never too old to learn, never too late to turn
- New brooms sweep clean
- No gains without pains
- No living man, all things can
- Nothing succeeds like success

- Old wounds soon bleed
- One fool makes many
- One may lead a horse to the water, but twenty cannot make him drink
- One man's meat is another man's poison
- One swallow does not make a summer
- One today is worth two tomorrows
- Penny wise, pound foolish
- Practise thrift else you will drift
- Presents keep friendship warm
- Prevention is better than cure
- Put not your trust in money; put your money in trust
- Rumour is a great traveller
- Saying is one thing, doing another
- Second thoughts are best
- Seeing is believing
- Silence gives consent
- Small beginnings make great endings
- Sympathy without relief is mustard without beef
- Soft words win hard hearts
- The less people think the more they talk
- The master's eye fattens the horse
- The wise make jests and fools repeat them
- There is a "But" in everything
- There is no true love without jealousy
- There is no venom like that of the tongue
- Two wrongs do not make a right as two blacks do not make a white
- What belongs to everybody belongs to nobody
- An honest man will marry soon but a wise man never

- What can't be cured must be endured
- What's done can't be undone
- What man has done man can do
- What the eye does not admire the heart does not desire
- When poverty comes in at the door love flies out of the window
- Whom the God's love die young
- Wine and wenches empty men's purses

Words Pertaining to War

Aggression	an unprovoked attack by an enemy
Belligerent	nations carrying on warfare
Conscription	compulsory enrolment as soldiers or sailors
Convoy	a number of ships travelling under escort
Contraband	smuggling of goods
Détente	relaxation of strained relationship between two countries
Espionage	the act of spying
Evacuate	to remove from one place to another to avoid the destruction of war
Embargo	an order prohibiting ships to leave the port

Ordnance	heavy guns, artillery and army stores
Parole	a promise given by a prisoner not to try to escape if given temporary relief
Reveille	music for awakening soldiers in the morning
Volley	a shower of bullets
Salvo	the firing of many guns at the same time to mark an occasion
Cavalry	horse soldiers
Infantry	foot soldiers
Fusillade	a number of fire arms being discharged continuously
Reconnoiter	to make an examination or preliminary survey of enemy territory
Armistice	an agreement by belligerents to stop fighting
Annihilate	to reduce to nothing
Amnesty	a general pardon of offenders
Recruit	a soldier recently enlisted for service
Guerilla war	an irregular warfare conducted by scattered or independent bands
Commandeer	to seize for military use
Bivouac	an encampment in the open air

Foreign Phrases

Many of these foreign words and phrases are an intrinsic part of English usage. With the decline in teaching of languages in schools it becomes more important than ever to familiarise ourselves with the meaning and use of these words.

Agnus dei (Latin)	The Lamb of God
A la carte (French)	according to a menu, a selected menu in contrast to "table d'hote" – set meal of a hotel
Al fresco (Italian)	in the open air
Amor vincit omnia (Latin)	Love conquers all
Anno domini (Latin)	in the year of our lord
Annus mirabilis (Latin)	A year of wonders
Apologia (Greek)	a written justification of ones conduct and action
Aqua vitae (Latin)	literlliy, water of life i.e. brandy
Au revoir (French)	till we meet again
A fortiori (Latin)	literally, 'from yet firmer ground' or 'with stronger reason'

A priori (Latin)	literally, 'from the former'
A propos (French)	'to the point' or 'with reference to'
Ad infinitum (Latin)	'to infinity'
Alibi (Latin)	literally, 'elsewhere'. The term is originally a legal one; it refers to a plea in defence that the defendant seeks to prove that he was elsewhere at the time the crime was committed
Alma mater (Latin)	literally, 'bounteous mother'. The term is still used by graduates in referring to the university where they studied – thus school or university
Bambino (Italian)	a little boy often applied to the infant Jesus
Beau monde (French)	the fashionable world
Bella donna (Italian)	a pretty woman
Belles – letters (French)	literally, fine letters now essays or poems
Belle vue (French)	a fine prospect
Billet-doux (French)	a love letter

Bona fide (Latin)	in good faith, genuine
Bourgeoisie (French)	the term historically denotes the social class between the gentry and the labourers and artisans
Canard (French)	a rumour; a hoax
Chef-d'oeuvre (French)	master piece
Cheri (French)	beloved
Corrigendum (Latin)	corrections in a book
Coup d'etat (French)	a swift stroke of policy
Coup de grace (French)	a finishing stroke; a death blow
Cuisine (French)	literally, kitchen; the kind of cooking produced
Carte blanche (French)	literally, 'a white paper', hence metaphorically 'an open invitation or complete permission'
Coup de grace (French)	finishing stroke
Curriculum vitae (Latin)	a record of one's life history
Double entendre (French)	a double meaning
Dulce domum (Latin)	home, sweet home

Dramatic personae (Latin)	the characters in a play
Ecce homo (Latin)	Behold the man! said by Pilate of Christ wearing the crown of thorns
Élan (French)	dash, spirit
Eldorado (Spanish)	the golden land of dreams
Elite (French)	the pick, the best
En masse (French)	in a body
Eureka (Greek)	I have it
Excelsior (Latin)	higher – the motto of New York
Ex-gratia (Latin)	an act of grace
Ex officio	by virtue of office
Ennui (French)	boredom, depression
Esprit de corps (French)	a spirit of unity and solidarity with one's comrades
Fainéant (French)	sluggard; do-nothing
Fin de siecle (French)	end of a century, decadent
Flair (French)	scent, sense of smell. Flair now in English means astuteness, an instinctive aptitude
Garcon (French)	waiter

Gloria in excelsis deo (Latin)	glory to God in the highest
Gratis (Latin)	free of charge, for nothing
Hotel de ville (French)	a town hall
Ibidem (ibid) (Latin)	in the same place; used for subsequent references
Ich dien (German)	I serve – the motto of the Prince of Wales
Ingénue (French)	a young, unsophisticated person
In status quo (Latin)	in its original state
Ipso facto (Latin)	in the fact itself; virtually
In loco parentis (Latin)	in the place of a parent
Laissez-faire (French)	non-interference especially in economic matters; let matters be
Lapsus celami (Latin)	a slip of the pen
Leit motif (German)	the recurring theme in a musical composition
Lingua franca (Italian)	any language spoken or understood by various people over a wide area
Matinee (French)	an afternoon performance

Modus operandi (Latin)	the way of working
Notre-dame (French)	our Lady
Par excellence (French)	pre-eminently
Piazza (Italian)	a public square
Pro forma (Latin)	as a matter of form
Post mortem (Latin)	after death
Quantum (Latin)	how much?
Rendezvous (French)	meeting place
Resume (French)	a summary or abstract
Sanctum sanctorum (Latin)	the holy of holies
Sine die (Latin)	indefinitely, without an appointed day
Sine qua non (Latin)	indispensable condition
Sub poena (Latin)	writ commanding one to attend a court of law
Soi disant (French)	self-styled
Status quo (Latin)	literally, 'the state in which'; hence, 'as things are or were'; as things were before

Tableu (French)	a picture; a set-piece
Tête-a-tete (French)	a private conversation between two persons
Tour de force (French)	a feat of strength or a performance of distinction
Ultima ratio regum (Latin)	the last argument of kings; i.e. war
Ultra vires (Latin)	beyond the powers possessed
Ut infra (Latin)	as below
Ut supra (Latin)	as above
Veni, vidi, vici (Latin)	I came, I saw, I conquered
Versus (Latin)	against
Via media (Latin)	a middle course
Vide (Latin)	see
Vis-à-vis (French)	face to face, opposite
Viva voce (Latin)	orally
Zeitgeist (German)	the spirit of the age

Some Important English Idioms

Adjective - Noun Phrases

A.B.C.	The first rudiments; the beginning

Abide by or with	Remain faithful to an agreement or decision
An absent-minded person	A person inattentive to what is going on around him at the moment.
A bolt from the blue	A sudden and entirely unexpected disaster
A blind alley	A narrow street or lane closed at one end.
A black sheep	One who has a bad reputation
A bosom friend	An intimate, trusted friend
A chip of the old block	One exhibiting the characteristics of his parents or ancestors
A chicken-hearted fellow	A timid, cowardly fellow
A close-fisted man	A stingy man, a miser
A close shave	Almost an accident
A damp squib	A joke or other form of entertainment which has failed
A dark horse	A person whose qualities and possibilities are unknown
A down train	Is a train which starts from the principal terminus of the railway. A train going towards the terminus is called an UP TRAIN.

A fatal blow	A blow causing death
A fair weather friend	One who deserts you in difficulties
A henpecked husband	A man habitually snubbed by his wife
A herculean task	Work requiring great effort for its accomplishment
Alert	On the alert. In a state of awareness
All in all	Everything
Apple-pie order	Perfectly tidy and neat
An honest penny	A small sum of money honestly earned
Air	Give oneself airs. Try to impress people with one's superiority
A pious fraud	A deception carried out under the plea of religion
A public house	A house licenced for the retail sale of alcoholic liquors
A rainy day	A time of adversity
A red letter day	An auspicious fortunate day
A sheet anchor	The chief support
A slow coach	A dull, stupid fellow
A wet blanket	A person whose presence checks enthusiasms

A white elephant	An unprofitable investment possession
A white lie	A harmless lie
A wild goose chase	A foolish, wild unprofitable adventure
Axe to grind	A private and personal object to achieve or favour to obtain
Bad blood	Ill-feeling; antagonism
Blue blood	Aristocratic or of gentle birth
Beggar's description	Be so extraordinary that one cannot find words in which to describe it.
Better half	Wife
Bone of contention	The subject of argument or dispute
Bring to book	Bring to justice; punish
Bread-winner	The person whose earnings support the family
Break the ice	Break an uncomfortable silence; put an end to stiffness
Bury the hatchet	Forget past quarrels, and become friends
Button-hole	Intercept and speak privately to
By and by	Soon, in the near future
Baker's dozen	Thirteen

Bread and butter letter	One written when a visit is over, thanking one's hostess
Capital punishment	The punishment of death legally inflicted
Cold war	Unfriendly relations between countries
Crocodile tears	Pretended sorrow
Call names	Abuse
Chequered career	One including many changes; successes and failures
Clap-trap	Worthless, valueless talk, generally used in an attempt to become popular or appear learned
Cupboard love	Affection shown only in the hope of obtaining something tangible in return
Curry favour	Attempt by flattery, bribery, etc. to become popular
Curtain lecture	Admonition – "nagging" by a wife to a husband at bedtime
Dutch courage	Temporary courage created by drinking
Elbow-room	Space in which to move
Filthy lucre	Money; wealth

Fast colours	Colours which do not fade or wash out
Fast living	Devotion to pleasure
Follow suit	Behave similarly; to do the same thing
Fool proof	So simple and strong that even a fool cannot use it wrongly or break it.
French leave	Abandon one's work or post without obtaining the necessary permission from one's superior
Goose flesh	A cold and roughened condition of the skin caused by fear or cold
Grease a man's palm	Bribe
Have qualms	Have doubts; feel uneasy
Hit below the belt	Attack unfairly
Hobson's choice	No choice at all
Hush money	A bribe paid to secure silence
In cold blood	Deliberately; coolly
In clover	In a condition of luxury
In the doldrums	Depressed and miserable
Lay an embargo on	A legal prohibition or apply definite impediments
Land slide (political)	A sudden complete change of political popularity

Leave in the lurch	Abandon in circumstances of danger and difficulty
Make a bee line	Proceed in a straight line, as a bee does on its way home
On behalf of	As a substitute for, or representative of, some one
Pass muster	Be regarded as up to the necessary standards; just good enough
Palmy days	Prosperous times
Piping hot	Quite hot, at great heat
Pull strings	Use private and personal influence
Point blank	Directly out of hand
Red tape	Excessive official formality
Salt of the earth	The best, most valuable members of society
Show down	A frank exposure; an open challenge
Sinews of war	Money
Stone blind	Completely blind
Stone deaf	Completely deaf
Strong drink	An alcoholic drink, e.g. brandy, whisky
Take pot luck	Accept impromptu hospitality without definite invitation

Wet blanket	A person who by his manner or conversation extinguishes the enthusiasm of others
Whet the appetite	Increase one's desire to eat
Win laurels	Acquire honour
White heat	Intense heat
Write off	Treat as no longer of any value
Yellow livered	Cowardly
Yeoman service	Sound and excellent work

Some Key Business Words

Best of Breed

e.g: If we're going to survive in this market, we'll need to challenge the best of breed.
Meaning: Our service is rubbish compared to our biggest competitors. Similar: Best in class.

Bespoke

e.g: We'll develop you a bespoke solution.
Meaning: We'll actually develop something specifically for you.

Big Hitter

e.g: I'm in awe of that Exec - he's a really big hitter.
Meaning: One powerful within the confines of the company.

Blue Sky Thinking

e.g: Let's start with a blank sheet of paper and do some blue sky thinking and see what happens.

Meaning: Think 'out of the box' and where you come up with ideas taking into account no preconceptions and not dismissing ideas instantly.

Brain Dump

e.g: Have a brain dump and see what you come up with.

Meaning: Brainstorm.

Core Competencies

e.g: We need to focus on our core competencies in order to maintain our edge in the marketplace.

Meaning: What you/your company does well.

Customer Centric

e.g: We need to be customer-centric from now on.

Meaning: customer driven.

Cutting Edge

e.g: This is cutting edge technology we're using.

Meaning: Most recent version.

End to End

e.g: Let's visualise the process end-to-end.

Meaning: Let's work out the whole process.

E.T.A.

e.g: What's the E.T.A. on this report?

Meaning: Expected time of arrival: time taken to get it finished.

First Mover

e.g: If we launch things now, we'll have first mover advantage.

Meaning: Massive advertising costs to have the advantage of getting lots of customers first.

Going Forward

e.g: I think it's important that, going forward, you continue to manage the project pro-actively.
Meaning: In the future.

Go To Market

e.g: We need to update our go-to-market strategy.
Meaning: How we will process to launch things.

High Level

e.g: Remember the more important you are, the more you're concerned with high level thinking.
Meaning: The big picture; taking an overall view rather than looking at the detail.

Joined Up

e.g From now on this company will only engage in joined up thinking.
Meaning: Looking at things from the wider point of view.

Leading (Market)

e.g: I want to develop a market leading proposition
Meaning: I want to develop something much better than our competitors.

Leverage (the Proposition)

e.g. See if you can leverage the proposition with them over point x and xx.
Meaning: Getting some value out of a certain situation and maximising the benefits.

Low Hanging Fruit

e.g. We started off by removing the low hanging fruit, before looking at the tougher problems.
Meaning: The bits that can be done quickly and easily but still have an effect.

Manage Expectations

e.g: Make sure that you manage expectations so that they're not disappointed if we can't deliver.
Meaning: Make sure people expect realistic outcomes from a project.

Mission Critical

e.g: This project is mission critical.
Meaning: If things don't work out we are in big trouble.

On the Planet

e.g. This is the greatest product on the planet.
Meaning: The very best of the best.

Out of the box

e.g. It'd be great if you could think out of the box on this.
Meaning: Not the same old solutions, try and be creative.

Out of Pocket

e.g.: I'll be out-of-pocket on this project.
Meaning: I will have to pay from my own money.

Pro-active

e.g.: I think we need to be a bit pro-active here.
Meaning: Take the initiative and take action, do not wait.

Push Back

e.g: Can you just push back on that point and get him to amend his position?

Meaning: Try to get someone to change their mind, or debate a point, by questioning their opinion.

Quick Win

e.g: Please come up with a list of quick wins.

Meaning: Things that can be done quite easily with positive results.

Robust

e.g: Before taking this to market, let's make sure it's robust.

Meaning: Let's be sure it doesn't break down within the first few months.

Scalable

e.g: It's a great solution for 100 customers, but is it scalable?

Meaning: Will it work for lots of people as well as just a few?

Seamless

e.g: Ideally, our customers would experience a seamless proposition.

Meaning: Our customers want one, easy relationship with us no matter how they contact us

Solutions

e.g.: Let's come up with some solutions for this situation.

Meaning: Let's focus on what can be done to solve the problem.

Space

e.g: There's a lot going on in the moment in that space.
Meaning: There's a lot of activity in that area in that moment.

State of the Art

e.g: This is great - it's a state of the art solution.
Meaning: Really good, the best, most modern solution.

Take offline

e.g: I think that's a separate issue, so can you take it offline, please?
Meaning: Discuss the point further outside the meeting / at another time.

Take ownership

e.g: I think it's up to you to really take ownership of the piece of work.
Meaning: You need to be responsible for the piece of work.

Team Player

e.g: The manager from accounts is a real team player.
Meaning: Someone who is not just out for themselves but works well with others.

The Big Picture

e.g: I think it's important that we remember to look at the big picture
Meaning: The overall situation

The New World
e.g: In the new world, things will look a little different.
Meaning: What things will be like in the future after change.

Touch Base
e.g: "I need to touch base with Govil on this one."
Meaning - "I need to go a speak to Govil about this."

Traction
e.g.: I'm concerned. We're working hard, but not getting much traction on this.
Meaning: Despite our best efforts, we are not making progress as we should be.

Turnkey
e.g: I'm looking for a turnkey solution.
Meaning: A solution that does it all and is complete to go.

Upskill
e.g: During your career it's important to ensure you continue to upskill .
Meaning: It is a good idea to develop and improve your skills.

Win win
e.g.: Try and see if you can come up with a win-win situation.
Meaning: A situation that is good for people on both sides.

GENERAL MEDIA TERMS

- Advertising Impressions: Audience delivery of media vehicles, programmes or schedules. Also thousands (000).
- Advertising Research Foundation (ARF): A non-profit organisation of advertisers.
- Advertising Weight: Level of advertising support over a period of time.
- Aided Recall: A research technique as an aid to help remember advertising.
- As It Falls: Media test market.
- Average Frequency: Gross Rating Points and Reach.
- Barter: Advertising was paid for by the advertiser using goods and services rather than cash.
- BDI (Brand Development Index): Strength of a brand's sales in a particular geographic area.
- CDI (Category Development Index): A brand's sales potential using sales of all brands within a category in a specific market.
- Clutter: Advertising messages aimed at consumers. In TV, it refers to all non-programme minutes, such as commercials, station promotions, billboards, public service announcements, etc.
- Cost Per Rating Point (Cost Per Point, CPP, Cost Per GRP): Cost to reach one percent

households or individuals, in a given market or geographic area.
- ♦ Cost Per Thousand (CPM): Cost to reach 1,000 units of audience, households or individuals, for advertising.
- ♦ Coverage Area: Specific geography where a media vehicle has its coverage.

BROADCAST MEDIA TERMS

- ♦ Adjacency: Commercial break positions.
- ♦ Affidavit: A statement, usually notarised that the commercial actually ran at the time stated on the invoice.
- ♦ Affiliate: A station associated with a network by contract to broadcast the network's programmes.
- ♦ Air Date: The first broadcast of a commercial.
- ♦ Audilog: The diary used for local rating sample which records what stations and programmes they viewed during a week's time.
- ♦ Audimeter: Device for electronically recording TV viewing in sample households.
- ♦ Average Quarter-Hour Rating: It provides the average number of persons or households who watched/listened for at least 5 minutes of the 15 minute segment being reported.
- ♦ Bonus Spot: Additional TV or radio spot provided to an advertiser at no charge to raise the overall audience delivery of the schedule.

- Break Position: A broadcast commercial aired between two programs instead of in the middle of one programme.
- Broadcast Calendar: An industry-accepted calendar used mainly for accounting and billing purposes.
- Cable TV: TV programming that is delivered by coaxial cable.
- Clearance: A station's agreement to carry a particular programme.
- Cut-In: A commercial inserted by the local station that covers the commercial airing at the same time on the network at the advertiser's request.
- Daypart: One of the time segments into which the day is divided by broadcast media.
- Designated Market Area (DMA): Based on which home market stations receive the predominant share of viewing.
- Diary: An instrument for measuring viewing, listening or reading of media vehicles kept by people in a sample.
- Drive Time: The day parts used in radio to signify primary listening being done in cars. Generally considered to be Monday-Friday 6-10 a.m. and 3-7 p.m.
- HUT (Households Using Television): A broadcast research term indicating the percent of homes with sets on during a specific time period.
- ID: Station identification of its call letters and location, channel or frequency.

- **Infomercial:** A long (more than two minutes) commercial providing extensive product/service description and sales information.
- **Log:** Chronological record of a station's program and commercial exact air times.
- **Network:** Two or more stations joined by a line to broadcast the same programme from a few original studios simultaneously.
- **Network Affiliate:** A television or radio station that designates a portion of its air time for network programmes.
- **O & O Station:** A station owned and operated by a network.
- **O.T.O.:** One time only, usually referring to a TV or radio special programme.
- **Overnights:** Audience data-metered market clients the day after the broadcast.
- **Pay Per View:** A type of Pay TV where viewers are charged each time they watch the special event or movie being broadcast.
- **Pay TV:** A TV system providing programmes which are available only to the households who subscribe, usually transmitted via coaxial cable or telephone lines. Also called "premium channels" on cable.
- **Persons Using Radio (PUR):** The percent of the area's population listening to radio at a specific time.
- **Piggyback:** Back-to-back scheduling of two or more brand commercials of one advertiser in network or spot positions.
- **Pilot:** A sample of a proposed television series.

- **Pocketpiece:** Weekly reports providing audience estimates for all network and syndicated programmes.
- **Pre-emption:** The substitution of one advertiser's local TV commercial by another advertiser paying a higher price for the spot.
- **PVT/PUT (Persons Viewing or Using Television):** The percent of individuals viewing all television stations during a specific time period.
- **Roadblocking:** A scheduling technique where a brand's commercial airs at approximately the same time on all three networks or on all stations in a given market.
- **R.O.S. (Run Of Schedule or Run Of Station):** A broadcast schedule.
- **Simulcast:** Broadcast of the same programme at the same time on both AM and FM radio stations.
- **Spill-In:** The amount of programming viewed within a market area to stations that are licenced to an adjacent market.
- **Spill-Out:** The amount of viewing to local stations outside the home market area.
- **Strip:** A programme scheduled at the same time each day, typically Monday-Friday.
- **Superstation:** An independent station whose signal is transmitted to many markets via a satellite.
- **Sweeps:** The 4-week periods when all TV markets are measured for station viewing and demographic information.

- ♦ Syndicated Programme: A programme bought by a station or advertiser from an independent organisation, not a network.
- ♦ TAP (Total Audience Plan): A radio schedule consisting of equal distribution of commercials across all major day parts.
- ♦ Turnover: The ratio of a cumulative audience to the average audience for a given period of time.
- ♦ Upfront: A term indicating that an advertiser has purchased advertising for the coming broadcast year in an early buying season, for the benefit of lower rates.
- ♦ Direct Response Advertising: Advertising message that calls for a prompt response to purchase a product or request more information.
- ♦ Duplication: Number or percent of the target audience in one media vehicle also exposed to another vehicle.
- ♦ Efficiency: The ratio of cost to size of audience used to compare media vehicles, plans or schedules.
- ♦ Exclusivity: An agreement whereby a media vehicle agrees to run no advertising directly competitive to the advertiser purchasing the media vehicle or programme.
- ♦ First Refusal: The opportunity for an advertiser to extend sponsorship rights of a programme or vehicle before it is offered to another advertiser.

- **Fixed Position:** An advertising position which remains fixed over time, such as the inside cover of a magazine.
- **Flighting:** A technique for extending advertising interspersed with periods of inactivity.
- **Flow Chart:** A calendar which dimensionalises media activity over time.
- **FY:** An abbreviation for fiscal year.
- **Gross Impressions:** The combined audiences of several media vehicles or several announcements within a vehicle.
- **Gross Rating Points (GRP's):** The sum of individual ratings in a media plan.
- **Guarantee:** A commitment to the advertiser by a medium that should audience delivery fall short of what was estimated, the advertiser will receive bonus.
- **Heavy-up:** An increase in advertising activity for a limited period of time.
- **Hiatus:** A scheduled period of inactivity between advertising flights.
- **Mail-Order Advertising:** Type of advertising in which the complete sales transaction takes place through the mail.
- **Makegood:** Comparable unit of advertising offered at no charge when the original spot or ad did not run or ran incorrectly.
- **Mediamark Research Inc. (MRI):** A syndicated research source measuring print and broadcast media audiences and product / brand usage profiles.

- Net Cost: Advertising rates which do not include advertising agency commission and/or include discounts.
- Penetration: Effectiveness of advertising's impact on consumers.
- Per Inquiry (P.I.): Agreement between a media owner and an advertiser where the advertiser pays the owner for advertising on the basis of the number of inquiries or completed sales from the advertising.
- Psychographic: Describes consumers on the basis of some psychological trait, characteristics or lifestyle.
- Quintile: The division of the audience or sample into five equal groups ranging from heaviest to lightest amount of exposure to any medium.
- Rate Card: A statement by a medium showing advertising costs, issue dates, programme names, closing dates, requirements, cancellation dates, etc.
- Rating: An estimate of the size of an audience expressed as one percent of the total population.
- Reach: The unduplicated percent of a potential audience exposed to advertising one or more times during a given period.
- Roll Out: An advertising technique where advertising is expanded to cover more and more markets as distribution/ product sales are also expanded.
- Share: The percent of an audience tuned to a particular programme at a given time.

- ♦ Share of Voice (SOV) A brand's percent of the total advertising weight in its product category.
- ♦ Short Rate: The cost difference between the discounted contract rate and the higher rate actually earned by an advertiser if he fails to fulfill the contracted amount of advertising.
- ♦ Sponsorship: Purchase of all or part of a TV programme or all pages of a magazine.
- ♦ Standard Rate & Data Service (SRDS): Monthly reports of publications, TV and radio stations' rate cards.
- ♦ Vehicle: Anything capable of exposing advertising to customers.

INTERNET MEDIA TERMS

Bookmark
A routine that allows you to save a reference to a site or page that you have already visited; refers to a feature of Netscape Navigator (a web browser) that allows you to collect and organise bookmarks of your favourite web sites.

Browser
An application used to view and navigate the World Wide Web and other Internet resources.

Browser War
A catch phrase that refers to the battles between Netscape and Microsoft for dominance of the web browser market.

Bug
Problem with computer software or hardware that causes it to malfunction or crash.

Bulletin Board System (BBS)
An open computer system that members can dial into in order to send email, join discussion groups, and download files.

Chat
A form of interactive online communication that enables typed conversations to occur in real-time.

Chat History
A transcript of a chat session.

Commercial Online Service
A computer network that supplies its members with access to chat rooms, bulletin boards, and other online content on a monthly fee basis.

Congestion
A state occurring in a part of a network when the message traffic is so heavy that it slows down network response time.

Connection
When two computers have established a path through which the exchange of information can occur.

Cookies
Small files that are downloaded to your computer when you browse certain web pages.

Copy Protection
A software lock placed on a computer program by its developer to thwart piracy.

Cracker
A malicious hacker who breaks (or cracks) the security of computer systems in order to access, steal, or destroy sensitive information.

Crossload
To send an attached file via email.

Domain Name
The official name of a computer connected to the Internet.

Domain Name System (DNS)
A database system which looks up host IP addresses based upon domain names.

Download
To transfer data from a larger "host" system to a smaller "client" system's hard drive or other local storage device.

Download Charges
Monetary charges associated with downloading a file from a commercial online service.

E-cash
Electronic money.

E-form
An electronic form that is filled out by a user and sent over a network.

Emoticon
Used to express emotions without words. For example, this winking face ;-) indicates "I'm joking", this sad face :-(expresses sadness or "I'm sulking". Also known as a "smiley".

Encryption
A procedure that renders the contents of a message or file unintelligible to anyone not authorised to read it.
PGP (Pretty Good Privacy) is a commonly-used encryption program.

Eyeballs
A viewing audience for a WWW site.

Facilitated Chat
In a facilitated chat, a host or facilitator controls the messages that appear on the chat screen.

FAQ
Acronym for Frequently Asked Questions.

Flame
A public post or email message that expresses a strong opinion or criticism.

Flame Bait
An inflammatory post that is designed to provoke a flame war or flame responses.

Flame on / Flame off
Notifiers that surround a flame message and let readers know that the message they are reading is a flame.

Flame War
A series of public posts in which people flame one another rather than contribute useful information.

Forum
Focused discussion group or area.

Go Word
The word associated with a forum or area on a commercial online service that allows you to get to that place quickly.

Hacker
An expert programmer who likes to spend a lot of time figuring out the finer details of computer systems or networks, as opposed to those who learn only the minimum necessary.

Handle
A nickname used in online communications.

Hit
A single user accessing a single file from a web server.

Home Page
A web page that is topically the main source of information about a particular person, group, or concept.

Host
1. A computer that allows users to communicate with other host computers on a network.
2. A chat term for someone who is managing a chat.

Hyperlink
A highlighted word or picture within a hypertext document that when clicked takes you to another place within the document or to another document altogether.

Hypertext
Text that includes links or shortcuts to other documents, allowing the reader to easily jump from one text to related texts, and consequentially from one idea to another, in a non-linear fashion.

Hypertext Markup Language (HTML)
The tag-based ASCII language used to create pages on the World Wide Web.

Hypertext Transfer Protocol (HTTP)
The protocol used by the World Wide Web to transfer HTML files.

Icon
A small graphic image that represents a file or application and when clicked upon produces a programmed result.

Iconographer
A skillful designer who elevates icon design to an art form.

Identity Hacking
Posing as someone else.

Infobahn
A variant of information superhighway.

Integrated Services Digital Network (ISDN)
A technology offered by telephone carriers that allows for the rapid transfer of voice and data.

Internet
A worldwide network of networks that all use the TCP/IP communications protocol and share a common address space..

Internet Explorer
A free web browser application from Microsoft.

Internet Relay Chat (IRC)
A chat network that operates over the Internet.

Internet Service Provider (ISP)
1. A business that delivers access to the Internet, usually for a monthly fee. 2. Any business that provides Internet services such as web sites or web site development.

InterNIC
The InterNIC is the entity that controls the registration of most domain names on the Internet.

Interoperability
The ability of software and hardware on multiple machines from multiple vendors to communicate meaningfully.

Intranet
A private network that uses Internet-related technologies to provide services within an organisation.

IP address
A string of four numbers separated by periods (such as 111.22.3.444) used to represent a computer on the Internet.

Jack In
To log in to a machine or connect to a network.

Java
Java is a device independent language, meaning that programs compiled in Java can be run on any computer.

JavaScript
A scripting language that allows lines of Java code to be inserted into HTML scripts.

Joint Photographic Experts Group (JPEG)
An image compression standard for still photographs that is commonly used on the web.

Kermit
A protocol used for transferring files over a dial-up connection.

Leased Line
A permanently established connection between computers over a dedicated phone line which is leased from a telephone carrier.

Line Noise
Static over a telephone line that interferes with network communications.

Link
A highlighted word or picture within a hypertext document that when clicked brings you to another place within the document or to another document altogether.

List Server
An automated mailing list distribution system.

Local Area Network (LAN)
A group of computers at a single location (usually an office or home) that are connected by phone lines or coaxial cable.

Mailbomb
The act of sending massive amounts of email to a single address with the malicious intent of disrupting the system of the recipient.

Mailing List
A discussion group that occurs via mass email distributions.

Mirror Site
A server which contains a duplicate of another WWW or FTP site.

Nanosecond
A measurement of time. There are 1,000,000,000 nanoseconds in a second.

Navigator
A web browser application from Netscape.

Net Surfing
Browsing or exploring a network or the World Wide Web to find places of interest.

Netiquette
Network etiquette, or the set of informal rules of behaviuor that have evolved in Cyberspace, including the Internet and online services.

Netlag
A condition that occurs on the Internet in which response time is greatly slowed due to heavy traffic.

Network
A group of computers or devices that are connected together for the exchange of data and sharing of resources.

Newsgroup
A public place where messages are posted for public consumption and response.

Online
Currently connected to a host, opposite of offline.

Password
A secret code that you utilise along with your user ID in order to log on to a network.

Path
The hierarchical description of where a directory, folder, or file is located on your computer or on a network.

Post
To send a message to a public area.

Postmaster
The name given to the person in charge of administrating email for a particular site.

Refresh
To clear the screen or part of the screen and redraw it again.

Remote Login
Operating a remote computer over a network as if it were a local computer.

Response Time
A measurement of the time between a request for information over a network and the network's fulfillment of that request.

Search Engine
A program or web site that enables users to search for keywords on web pages throughout the World Wide Web.

Security
Security means that viruses are prevented from infecting people's computer systems.

Server

A computer that provides information to client machines.

Shareware

Software that you can download from a network and "try before you buy."

Shouting

TYPING IN ALL CAPITAL LETTERS IS CONSIDERED SHOUTING IN ONLINE COMMUNICATIONS. Avoid this unless you really mean to shout.

Snail Mail

Regular postal mail, as opposed to email.

Sneakernet

The transfer of electronic information by physically carrying disks, tape, or some other media from one machine to another.

Spam

To send a message (usually an advertisement) to many discussion groups (bulletin boards, mailing lists, and / or newsgroups), without regard for its topical relevance.

Telecommunications

The science of sending signals representing voice, video, or data through telephone lines.

Telecommuting

To work at home and use a computer and modem to communicate with the office.

Thread

A series of postings on a particular topic.

Toggle
A switch that is either on or off.

Traffic
The load of packets carried by a network or portion of a network.

Triple-dub
An abbreivated way to say "WWW" when reciting a URL.

Upload
To send a file to a network.

Virus
An insidious piece of computer code written to damage systems.

Webliography
A listing of source World Wide Web sites.

Webmaster
The person in charge of administrating a World Wide Web site.

Worm
An insidious and usually illegal computer program that is designed to replicate itself over a network for the purpose of causing harm and / or destruction. While a virus is designed to invade a single computer's hard drive, a worm is designed to invade a network.

Print Media Terms

Audit Bureau of Circulations (ABC)
Organisation of publishers, advertising agencies and advertisers for verifying the circulation statements of member publications.

Advertising Checking Bureau (ACB)
A company which provides advertisers and agencies with newspaper tear sheets of ads, which have run.

Agate Line
A unit of measurement for newspaper advertising which measures one column wide with 14 agate lines per inch.

Bleed
A term used for print advertising that extends all the way to the edge of the page with no margin.

Business Publication Audit of Circulation (BPA)
An organisation for auditing the circulation of business (trade) publications.

Checkerboard
Magazine advertising that uses diagonal quarter or half page ads alternating with editorial.

Checking Copy
A copy of a publication sent to the advertiser and the agency as proof the ad ran as ordered.

Circulation
The total number of distributed copies of a publication at a specified time.

Closing Date
The date by which all advertising must be ordered from the specific media vehicle in order to secure the dates/times/positions requested.

Column Inch
A unit of newspaper space one column wide and one inch deep (14 agate lines).

Direct Mail Advertising
Any printed material sent through the mail directly to prospective customers.

Double Truck
A newspaper ad unit that uses two facing full pages, including the gutter or fold.

Gutter
The blank space between margins of facing pages of a publication.

Insertion Order
Written instructions from the advertiser or agency authorising a publication to run a specific advertisement in a specific issue.

Island Position
A print advertisement surrounded completely by editorial.

Line Rate
The cost per agate line for newspapers.

Magazine Supplement
The magazine section of a Sunday newspaper produced either locally or nationally.

Net Paid Circulation
A term used by ABC for the circulation of a publication for which at least 50% of the subscription or newsstand price has been paid.

PBW, P4C
Abbreviations for Page Black and White and Page Four Colour.

Pass-along Audience
Readers of magazines or newspapers who did not purchase the publication. Also called Secondary Audience.

Publishers Information Bureau (PIB)
A syndicated source of monthly reports on advertising activity in major consumer magazines, reported by product or service category.

Publisher's Statement
A notarised statement from the publisher of total circulation, geographic distribution, method of getting subscriptions, etc.

Readers Per Copy
Average number of readers for one copy of a newspaper or magazine.

Regional Edition
An edition of a national publication's circulation that falls in a certain geographic area for which advertising may be purchased separately, usually at a cost premium.

Remnant Space
Magazine space sold at reduced prices at the last minute when another advertiser's materials donot arrive or to fill out regional editions.

Run Of Press or Run Of Paper (ROP)

A newspaper insertion for which an exact position is not requested but left to the newspaper's discretion.

Split Run

Scheduling two or more executions of an advertising message in alternate copies of a magazine's circulation in a given issue.

Tabloid

A newspaper measuring about 5-6 columns wide by 200 lines deep, about 2/3 the size of a standard newspaper.

Spam Vocabulary

GLOSSARY OF SPAM TERMS:

Spam

All unsolicited commercial email (UCE) and unsolicited bulk email (UBE) that a recipient does not want to receive.

Address harvester

A program that searches web pages and filters newsgroup postings looking for valid email addresses to be used for spam purposes.

Bayesian filtering

A statistical approach to determine whether an email is spam.

Block list

A publicised list, usually commercial, of IP addresses known to be sources of spam, which can be used to create a network block list to filter out mail originating from these addresses.

Complex dictionary checking

A feature of anti-spam software that screens text for rude words and isn't fooled by various spam tricks, such as the replacement of letters with lookalike numerals or characters (such as "1nterest r@te").

CSS spam

Exploits Cascading Style Sheets (CSS), which are used to control the display of web pages, in order to conceal messages in spam.

Denial of Service (DoS) attack

Where a hacker sends attachments or other unusual or excessive traffic in an attempt to bring down email systems.

Dictionary attack

A program that bombards a mail server with millions of alphabetically generated email addresses in the hope that some addresses will be guessed correctly. This technique is also used to crack passwords.

Directory Harvest Attack (DHA)

When a spammer bombards a domain with thousands of generated email addresses in an attempt to collect valid email addresses from an organisation.

Domain Name System Block Lists (DNSBL)

Commercial lists of networks that either allow spammers to use their systems to send spam, or have not taken action to prevent spammers from abusing their systems.

False negative
When anti-spam software fails to identify a spam message as spam.

False positive
When anti-spam software wrongly identifies a legitimate message as spam.

Greylist
Senders who are not block-listed (excluded) or allow listed (accepted) can be placed on a greylist.

Hacker
Someone who intentionally breaches computer security, usually to cause disruption or gain confidential information such as financial details.

Ham
All email that a recipient does not consider to be spam.

Harvesting
The process of scanning the internet to identify email addresses in order to create lists for spamming.

Honeypot
A computer system on the Internet set up to attract and trap spammers and hackers.

Joe job
A Joe job is a spam campaign forged to appear as though it came from an innocent party, with the intention of incriminating or pinning blame on to that party.

Listwashing
The process of removing email addresses from a mailing list at the request of the recipients.

Mail drop
An email address set up to receive email resulting from spam sent from a different ISP. The spammer will cancel the account from which the spam originated in an attempt to avoid detection.

Munging
A technique to protect email addresses from harvesting by changing them and rendering them invalid.

Morph
A method that a spammer uses to avoid detection by anti-spam software, which involves modifying an email header.

Mousetrapping
A technique that page-jackers use, so that users tricked into visiting an illegitimate site encounter only additional, unwanted pages when they click the Back button to try to escape.

Network check (also known as reverse DNS check)
When an anti-spam engine uses a Domain Name System database to check an email's IP address to ensure that it originated from a valid domain name or web address.

Newsgroup
An electronic forum where readers post articles and follow-up messages on specified topics. Often

targeted by spammers seeking to harvest email addresses.

Obfuscation
Spammers' attempts to hide data to prevent its detection.

Opt-in
The process of agreeing to receive email from a business source.

Opt-out
The process of declining to receive email from a business source.

Page-jacking
This involves stealing the contents of a website by copying some of its pages, placing them on a site that appears to be legitimate.

Phishing
(Pronounced 'fishing'.) This involves creating a replica of a legitimate web page to hook users and trick them into submitting personal or financial information or passwords.

Phreaking
This involves illegally breaking into the telephone network to make free long-distance phone calls or to tap phone lines.

Ratware
Software that spammers use to automate spam campaigns, coordinate spam services, and generate, send and track spam messages.

Social engineering
Conning email recipients into opening messages,

revealing passwords or providing other confidential information.

Spambot
A program that spammers use to harvest email addresses from the Internet.

Spam trap
Spam trap is an email address set up by a spam fighter to capture unsolicited email ads for the purpose of tracking spammers.

Spoofing
When spammers forge an email address to hide the origin of a spam message.

Tarpitting
The use of traffic monitoring to identify remote IP addresses sending a suspiciously large volume of email.

Teergrube (or tarpit)
An intentionally slow server that aims to trap spammers using harvesting programs.

Web bug
A small graphic inserted in an email or web page that alerts a spammer when a message is read or previewed.

Zombie
An insecure web server or computer that is hijacked and used in a DoS attack or to send spam.

HOW YOU SAY

There are two canons that make a good and impressive speaker: 'What you say' and 'How you say'. Today almost everyone is a public speaker. The business man, the teacher, the student, the sales manager, the professional – almost every man and woman connected with any organisation – all are called upon to 'say a few words'. This brief collection will add spice and flavour to your presentation.

WIT & WISDOM OF FAMOUS PERSONS

A celebrity is a person who works hard all his life to become well known, and then wears Dark glasses to avoid being recognised. —*Fred Allen*

Let us be thankful for the fools. But for them the rest of us could not succeed. —*Mark Twain*

It's far easier to forgive an enemy after you've got even with him .—*Olin Miller*

When you're down and out, something always turns up—and it's usually the noses of your friends.
—*Orson Welles*

A friend that ain't in need is a friend indeed.
—*Kin Hubbard*

There's one way to find out if a man is honest—ask him. If he says, "Yes," you know he's a crook.
—*Groucho Marx*

Love doesn't make the world go round. Love is what makes the ride worthwhile.
—*Franklin P. Jones*

There are a terrible lot of lies going about the world, and the worst of it is that half of them are true. —*Winston Churchill*

The biggest liar in the world is They Say.

—*Douglas Malloch*

Memory is what tells a man that his wife's birthday was yesterday. —*Mario Rocco*

Middle age is when you're sitting at home on Saturday night and the telephone rings and you hope it isn't for you. —*Ogden Nash*

He had so much money that he could afford to look poor. —*Edgar Wallace*

I'd like to live like a poor man with lots of money.

—*Pablo Picasso*

The trouble with being punctual is that nobody's there to appreciate it. —*Franklin P. Jones*

It is a very sad thing that nowadays there is so little useless information. —*Oscar Wilde*

No author is a man of genius to his publisher.

—*Heinrich Heine*

Tact: Ability to tell a man he's open minded when he has a hole in his head. —*F.G. Kernan*

It is always the best policy to speak the truth, unless of course you are an exceptionally good liar.

—*Jerome K. Jerome*

I hate to see men overdressed; a man ought to look like he's put together by accident, not added up on purpose. —*Christopher Marley*

No one is exempt from talking nonsense; the misfortune is to do it solemnly.—Michel de Montaigne

Be nice to people on your way up because you'll meet them on your way down. —*Wilson Mizner*

Everything bows to success, even grammar.
—*Victor Hugo*

Youth is a blunder, manhood a struggle, old age a regret. —*Benjamin Disraeli*

There is always something about your success that displeases even your best friends. —*Mark Twain*

A hair in the head is worth two in the brush.
—*Oliver Herford*

Order is the first requisite of liberty.
—*George Wilhelm Hegel*

What a good thing Adam had — when he said a good thing, he knew nobody had said it before.
—*Mark Twain*

I can believe anything, provided it is incredible.
—*Oscar Wilde*

When I am dead, I hope it may be said:
"His sins were scarlet but his books were read."
—*Hilaire Belloc*

There is nothing that people get tired of so quickly as the things they like the most.
—*W. Burton Baldry*

He's the kind of bore who's here today and here tomorrow.
—*Binnie Barnes*

A bore is a fellow who opens his mouth and puts his feets in it.
—*Henry Ford*

Lend only what you can afford to lose.
—*George Herbert*

Do not put off till tomorrow what can be enjoyed today.
—*Josh Billings*

Middle age is when your age starts to show around your middle.
—*Bob Hope*

City life: millions of people being lonesome together.
—*Henry David Thoreau*

Talk to a man about himself and he will listen for hours.
—*Benjamin Disraeli*

Gardens are not made by singing "Oh, how beautiful" and sitting in the shade.
—*Rudyard Kipling*

There is no wealth but life.
—*John Ruskin*

No man has a good enough memory to make a successful liar.
—*Abraham Lincoln*

God often visits us, but most of the time we are not at home.
—*Joseph Roux*

Experience is the best of schoolmasters, only the school fees are heavy.
—*Thomas Carlyle*

Work is the greatest thing in the world, so we should always save some of it for tomorrow.
—*Don Herold*

Give us the luxuries of life and we will dispense with necessaries. —*Oliver Wendell Holmes*

If you keep your mouth shut, you will never put your foot in it. —*Austin O'Malley*

The road to success is filled with women pushing their husbands along. —*Lord Dewar*

My father taught me to work; he did not teach me to love it. —*Abraham Lincoln*

If you tell the truth, you don't have to remember anything. —*Mark Twain*

By all means marry; if you get a good wife, you'll become happy; if you get a bad one, you'll become a philosopher. —*Socrates*

The old believe everything, the middle-aged suspect everything, the young know everything.
—*Oscar Wilde*

Make yourself an honest man and then you may be sure there is one rascal less in the world.
—*Thomas Carlyle*

Middle age occurs when you are too young to take up golf and too old to rush up to the net.
—*Franklin P. Adams*

So much of what we call management consists in making it difficult for people to work.
—*Peter Drucker*

In a hierarchy every employee tends to rise to his level of incompetence. —*Laurence J. Peter*

When people are serving, life is no longer meaningless.
—*John Gardner*

Consistency is the last refuge of the unimaginative.
—*Oscar Wilde*

In his private heart no man much respects himself.—Mark Twain

To err is human, but when the eraser wears out ahead of the pencil, you're overdoing it.
—*J. Jenkins*

We learn from experience. A man never wakes up his second baby just to see it smile.
—*Grace Williams*

When I was young I used to think that money was the most important thing in life; now that I am old, I know it is.
—*Oscar Wilde*

Civilisation is a race between education and catastrophe.
—*H.G. Wells*

Genius may have its limitations, but stupidity is not thus handicapped.
—*Elbert Hubbard*

Silence is the unbearable repartee.
—*G.K. Chesterton*

A lover of himself, without any rival.
—*Cicero*

An empty stomach is not a good political adviser.
—*Albert Einstein*

Young men think old men are fools; but old men know young men are fools.
—*George Chapman*

When a man wants to murder a tiger, he calls it sport; when a tiger wants to murder him, he calls it ferocity. —*George Bernard Show*

Many a man in love with a dimple makes the mistake of marrying the whole girl.—*Stephen Leacock*

The young may die, but the old must!
—*Henry Wadsworth Longfellow*

I have been laid up with intentional flu.
—*Samuel Goldwyn*

To love oneself is the beginning of a lifelong romance. —*Oscar Wilde*

Experience is the name everyone gives to his mistakes. —*Oscar Wilde*

You can't set a hen in one morning and have chicken salad for lunch. —*George Humphrey*

The art of being a good guest is to know when to leave. —*Duke of Edinburgh*

The most popular labour saving device today is still a husband with money. —*Joey Adams*

Every man's life is a fairy tale written by God's fingers. —*Hans Christian Andersen*

Literature was formerly an art and finance a trade: today it is the reverse. —*Joseph Roux*

In love, one first deceives oneself and then others— and that is what is called romance.
—*John L. Balderston*

Nobody in love has a sense of humour.

—*S.N. Behrman*

Love is like the measles; we all have to go through it. —*Jerome K. Jerome*

We must believe in luck. For how else can we explain the success of those we don't like?

—*Jean Cocteau*

The best audience is one that is intelligent, well educated—and a little drunk. —*Alben W. Barkley*

Fastest way for a politician to become an elder statesman is to lose an election. —*Earl Wilson*

I believe if we introduced the Lord's Prayer here, Senators would propose a large number of amendments to it. —*Senator Henry Wilson*

After being turned down by numerous publishers, he decided to write for posterity. —*George Ade*

One of the strangest things about life is that the poor, who need money the most , are the very one that never have it. —*Finley Peter Dunne*

We prefer the old-fashioned alarm clock to the kind that awakens you with soft music or a gentle whisper. If there's one thing we can't stand early in the morning, it's hypocrisy. —*Bill Vaughan*

Satire lies about literary men while they live, and eulogy lies about them when they die. —*Voltaire*

Ten years ago the moon was an inspiration to poets and young sweethearts; ten years from now it will be just another airport. —*Rep. Carroll Kearns*

Silence is one of the hardest arguments to refute.
—*Josh Billings*

The only way to get rid of a temptation is to yield to it. —*Oscar Wilde*

Women like silent men. They think they are listening. —*Marcel Achard*

Never buy anything with a handle on it. It means work. —*H. Allen Smith*

If you steal from one author, it's plagiarism; if you steal from many, it's research. —*Wilson Mizner*

Pleasure is frail like a dewdrop, while it laughs it dies. —*Rabindranath Tagore*

A good husband should be deaf and a good wife blind. —*French proverb*

Marriage is a mistake every man should make.
—*George Jessel*

History is simply a piece of paper covered with print; the main thing is still to make history, not to write it. —*Prince Otto von Bismarck*

Hope is merely disappointment deferred.
—*W. Burton Baldry*

Don't forget until too late that the business of life is not business, but living. —*B.C. Forbes*

Do you know the difference between a beautiful woman and a charming one? A beauty is a woman you notice; a charmer is one who notices you.
—*Adlai*

Poor men want meat for their stomachs, rich men stomachs for their meat. —*Anthony Copley*

Modern art is what happens when painters stop looking at girls and persuade themselves that they have a better idea. —*John Ciardi*

There are two kinds of people in one's life—people whom one keeps waiting, and the people for whom one waits... —*S.N. Behrman*

And More

Ability

It's not so much what we have, as what we do with what we have, that makes the difference in this world.

There is something that is much more scarce, something more than ability. It is the ability to recognise ability.

Adversity

Happy is the man who resolves that no matter how much life may confuse or wound him, it will, in the end bless him.

Advertising

Advertising is legalised lying.

Age

James Barrie was once asked how he managed to grow old so gracefully. He smiled as he an-

swered, "My dear lady, I give all my time to it."
It is not how old you are, but how you are old that counts. – Middle age is when the middle starts showing.
The sign that you are growing old is when the candles cost more than the cake.

Ancestors

An old proverb declares: "The man who has not anything to boast about but his glorious ancestors can be compared to a potato: the best part of him is underground.

Art

Art is not a thing, it is a way.
There are three forms of visual art:
Painting is art to look at, Sculpture is art you can walk around, architecture is art you can walk through.
Painting is silent poetry, and poetry is painting that speaks.

Atheist

An insightful man once defended an atheist with these words: "An atheist is a man who has no invisible means of support."

Atom

History is a short trudge from Adam to Atom.

Awareness

It took an unknown author to point out that happiness is sometimes in our backyard:

He searched the wide world over
To find a four-leafed clover
Which all the while had grown beside his door.

Bank

A place that lends you money only when you can prove that you don't need it.

Beauty

These things are beautiful beyond things:
The pleasant weakness that comes after pain,
The radiant greenness that comes after rain,
The deepened faith that follows after grief
And the awakening to love again.

Bible

"Don't just own a Bible; read it.
Don't only read it; understand it.
Don't only understand it; believe it.
Don't only believe it; live it."

Blessing

More than seven centuries ago, St. Francis of Assisi composed this beautiful prayer:
Where there is hatred, let me sow lover
Where there is injury, pardon;
Where there is doubt, faith;
Where there is despair, hope;
Where there is darkness, light;
Where there is sadness, joy.

Challenge

A man engendered his own life to rescue a small boy from drowning. The boy said, "Thank you, sir, for saving me." The man replied, "That's all right son. Just be sure you are worth saving."

Children

There are three ways to do a job: First, do it yourself; Hire a man to do it; the easiest – ask your children not to do it !
There is an oriental philosopher who once said that parents who are afraid to "put their foot down" usually have children who step on toes.

Conversation

The best recipe for the art of conversation comes from the Arabic. The pupil asked the sage how he could be a good conversationalist. "Listen, my son," replied the sage, holding up an admonishing finger. "I am listening, father," said the pupil after a silence. "Continue your instruction." " There is no more to tell," replied the sage.

Courage

Reinhold Niebuhr, the famous theologian wrote the following little prayer in 1934:
"Oh God, give us—
Serenity to accept what cannot be changed
Courage to change what should be changed
And the wisdom to distinguish the one from the other."

Criticism

The strongest foundation to success can be built by the bricks thrown at us by others.

Cynic

The cynic loves the world with a terrible hate
The saint hates the world with a terrible love.

Desire

"There are two tragedies in life," wrote George Bernard Shaw. "One is not to get your heart's desire. The other is to get it."

Discontent

As a rule a man's a fool,
When it's hot he wants it cool,
When it's cool he wants it hot
Always wanting what is not.

Education

The famous Greek philosopher, Aristotle said, "They who educate children well, are more to be honoured than they who produce them: for these only gave him life, those the art of living.

Ego

When two egotists meet, it results in a tie:
A vocal dead heat,
With an I for an I.

Elections

Elections are won by men and women chiefly because most people vote against somebody rather than for somebody.

Faith

Perhaps the most beautiful reply to "what is faith?" was given by a young child who answered, "Faith is doing God's will, and asking no questions."

Falsehood

When Aristotle was asked what a man could gain by telling a falsehood, he replied "Never to be credited when he speaks the truth."
A lie can travel half around the world while the truth is still putting on its shoes.

Failure

Failure is the condiment that gives success its flavour.

Fame

The heights by great men reached and kept
Were not attained by sudden flight
But they while their companions slept
Were toiling upward in the night.

Fanatic

A fanatic is a person who sticks to his guns although he knows for sure that he has no bullets.

Friendship

We have heard many definitions of a friend but none is more true than offered by a little boy: "A person who knows us – and still likes us."

Good

The word 'good' has many meanings for e.g., if a man were to shoot his grandmother at a range of 500 yards, I should call him a good shot, but necessarily not a good man. - G.K. Chesterton

The good die young – because they see it is no use living if you have got to be good. That which is beautiful may be goods but that which is good is always beautiful.

Gossip

It takes an enemy and a friend, working together, to hurt you to the heart. The one to slander you, and the other to get the news to you.

Gossip is the art of saying nothing in a manner that leaves nothing unsaid.

Happiness

Happiness is the interval between periods of unhappiness.

Happiness is a way station between 'too much' and 'too little'.

Happiness makes up in heights what it lacks in length.

History

History is a cyclic poem written on the memory of man.

History is a set of lies agreed upon.

History is a bucket of ashes.

Habit

There are four good habits – punctuality, accuracy, steadiness and dispatch. Without the first of these, time is wasted; without the second, mistakes occur; without the third, nothing can be well done; and without the fourth, opportunities of great advantage are lost.

Home

An artist who wanted to paint the most beautiful picture in the world, asked a pastor, "What is the most beautiful thing in the world?" "Faith" answered the pastor. The artist asked a young bride the same question. "Love", she replied. A weary soldier said "Peace is the most beautiful thing in the world". Faith, love and peace! How can I paint them? Thought the artist. Entering his door he saw faith in the eye of his children, and love in the eyes of his wife. And there in his home was the peace that love and faith had built. So he painted the most beautiful thing in the world. And, when he finished, he called it "HOME".

Inflation

Going to the market with a lot of money and yet being broke.

Leadership

There are two types of executives:
The boss drives his men; the leader coaches them.
The boss depends upon authority; the leader on goodwill
The boss inspires fear; the leader inspires enthusiasm.

The boss says "I"; the leader, "we".
The boss fixes the blame for the breakdown; the leader fixes the breakdown.
The boss says "Go"; the Leader says "Let's go".
The politician thinks of the next election; the statesman thinks of the next generation.

Lectures

A speech that's full of sparkling wit
Will keep its hearer grinning,
Provided that the end of it
Is close to the beginning.

Life

A professor of English prescribed a set of rules for adequate living, which he called "The Grammar of Life". He said:

Live in the active voice, not the passive. Think more about what you make happen than what happens to you.

Live in the indicative mood, rather than in the subjunctive.

Be concerned with things as they are, rather than as they might be.

Live in the present tense, facing the duty at hand without regret for the past or worry for the future.

Live in the singular number, caring more for the approval of your own conscience than for the applause of the crowd.

And, if you want a verb to conjugate, you cannot do better than to take the verb to love.

Love

If you don't feel just right,
If you can't sleep at night,
If you moan and you sigh,
If your throat feels dry,
If your food makes you choke,
If your heart doesn't beat,
If you're getting cold feet,
If your head's in a whirl –
Why not marry the girl?

There are three ways to curse a friend: Let him buy a race horse; let him buy a second hand car; let him fall in love. In all the three cases – he cannot SLEEP!

Man

Man can be divided into three categories: fits, misfits, and counterfeits.
Fits are those people who fit into society and do the job they have set out to do.
Misfits are those who are trying to do a job they do not know how to do.
Counterfeits are those who try to give the impression they are doing a job when in truth they are doing nothing.

Marriage

Marriage is not a word – it's a sentence.
Before he is married, married, man yearns for woman; after he is wed, the 'y' is silent.
The best way to spell marriage is – MIRAGE!

A man is really incomplete until he marries – then he is finished.
Love is blind but marriage is an eye-opener.

Memory

Memory is a crazy woman that hoards coloured rags and throws away food.
Every man's memory is his private literature.

Middle age

Middle age is – when you begin to smile at things that used to cause you to laugh.
Middle age is when you're sitting at home at Saturday night and the telephone rings and you hope it isn't for you.
Middle age is when you stop criticising the older generation and start criticising the younger.

Money

Money – in its absence we are coarse; in its presence we are vulgar.
Money is the sacrament of duty.
A lot of people say that to be too rich makes a man unhappy but it is not for this reason that many people are poor.
In order to be clever enough to earn a lot of money, one must be stupid enough to want to earn a lot.

Neighbours

Good fences make good neighbours – Robert Frost.

In the Bible it is written that we must love our enemy and our neighbour precisely because they happen to be the same person !

Silence

Professor Albert Einstein gave what he considered the best formula for success in life: If "a" is success in life, I should say the formula is a $x + y + z$, "x" being work and "y" being play." And what is 'z'? inquired the interviewer. "That", he answered, "is keeping your mouth shut."

Silence is one of the hardest arguments to refute.

Speakers

A wise man reflects before he speaks; a fool speaks, and then reflects on what he has said.

Tongue

A wit once said, "The tongue, being in a wet place, is bound to slip once in a while."

Women

All women are biased – yes BUY us this and BUY us that.

If you want to keep the female audience silent, just ask who is the oldest among them.

The minds of women are cleaner than those of men, because they are changed more often.

Words

Sartre in WORDS wrote: words are like centipedes – they catch us unawares.

Dr. Wilfred Funk's list of the ten most expressive words in the English Language is as follows:
The most bitter word is alone
The most reverent is mother
The most tragic is death
The most beautiful is love
The most cruel is hate
The most peaceful is tranquil
The saddest is forgotten
The warmest is friendship
The coldest is no
The most comforting is faith

And Now It's – One Word More.
Add Words as They Come into UsaGe